Prai

Inspirational! Your life is proof
there is a good God Who loves us dearly.
Your journey was not easy
and many of us can relate.
You are honest and show your flaws.
God even used your shortcomings
for His glory.

Georgina Khan
Cape Town, South Africa

Inspiring and good for the soul!

Janet S. Bivens-Neese
Texas

Your writings are profound
and really make me think
(sometimes in a totally
different way).

Sandra Melgren
California

What David has gone through could only come
from God. His illustrations hit home
and make you think.

Kevin Trimble
Indiana

Not only refreshing, but highly anointed!

Janae Shackelford
Kansas

Intellectual and thought-provoking!

Daniel Payne
Illinois

I love each and everything you write.
It gives hope to the hopeless!
Denise Ewing
Pennsylvania

David has done a lot of soul searching along with deep reflection about what he has overcome to crawl from the depths of despair and into the arms of a loving Savior.
He had faith in One he could not see, yet trusted Him to guide his way.
Rev. Steven Garner
Florida

Beautiful, enlightening, encouraging!
Marktin Birtcher
Arkansas

I am new to your page, and it was how well-written you are that brought me here. I love the way you write, and the content in a good read!
Vicky Gazaway
Mississippi

A bright spot in my day, your musing is very raw, real, and right to the point, and makes me dig deeper into the depths of God's love!
Paula Jeanne Lyons
Tennessee

Well written
and a blessing to all readers!
Dave Ducker
Inverness, Scotland

It's really simple.
Since I found the Baker and the Bread on Facebook, I am now in all of the related groups. I look forward to reading all of the chats and prayers daily. They are all inspiring, encouraging, and positive. Great Christian family, and I am so glad they accepted me!

Johnathan Stringer
Texas

Since I have found his writing,
my faith has stretched!
I have grown in the Spirit.
His encouragement to me personally
has meant so much in the past year.
God bless this younger brother
as he goes forward in his journey
to reach the Forgotten Ones!

Charlene J. McCaa
Louisiana

I always find your writings
refreshing and helpful!

Margarita Cordero
Texas

A must-read for anyone who wants to see
how God can turn a life around
from the most dire of circumstances!
He can change your life
from despair to repair,
with unexpected blessings sprinkled
along the way.
Our God is so good!

Di Speer
Texas

Beginnings

The Baker's Story
My Saga

Prequel to the Prelude

David W. Riordan

Beginnings

The Baker's Story
My Saga

ISBN: 979-8-9892190-0-1

Published by The Baker and the Bread
Chelsea, OK – TheBakerandtheBread.com

Dedication

I dedicate this book

to the Baker—
my Lord and Savior, Jesus Christ,

to my children who know what it means
better than most,

and

to M.
and everyone like her
who only want to know God
as I do.

Contents

Book 1

Book 2

FOREWORD

It never ceases to amaze me how our God brings people into our lives to fulfill His plans, plans that we don't always understand at the outset until we have an "Aha!" moment in which His perfect plan becomes crystal clear.

David Riordan is one of those people in my life. He came into my life through, of all things, Facebook. Social media does have its place in today's fast-paced world. Despite Facebook's often negative encounters, the Baker and the Bread and the team of people I've met through David are the real thing. They are genuine people who love the Lord, tasked with helping those forgotten by this world. His story is gripping and heart-wrenching and will ensnare you from the get-go. It certainly was the case for me. When I finished one chapter, I couldn't wait to discover how the story ended. As I continued reading, my heart was bereft not only with grief but also wholly disheartened by the treatment he had endured at the hands of the authorities.

I was humbled when he asked me to write the forward for this book. I became his friend by working with him and the rest of the team to get the Forgotten Ones Crusade going and this riveting book completed. What floored me is that, despite his justifiable distrust of law enforcement, he entrusted me with this incredible honor, especially given my background as a law enforcement officer, now retired. Talk about irony!

And yet, here we are. Thank you, David, for your trust. This is a book you won't be able to put down. His words will mesmerize you, and you will see his heart and how God has used his past to reach those with whom he would have had no credibility unless he had walked in the same shoes and truly understood it from the inside.

The choice is yours. I encourage you to read it. You won't regret the decision. I know I didn't.

Deidre Beiter
Chief of Police (Retired)
Spring City Police Department (Pennsylvania)

Author's Note

"Dee," as her friends knew her, was a bright light of encouragement and joy. I was humbled when she joined our ministry team. As you'll soon discover, I have my reasons. Facing stage four cancer for the second time, she worked online tirelessly from her perch in Pennsylvania. Like most of our team members, I never had a chance to meet her in person before the Forgotten Ones Crusade began, but she volunteered in every way she could.

When we formed the editing team for this book, she was first in line. She knew me well and learned much more, and it seemed odd to her, but like a well-composed musical piece, the contrapuntal harmonies of our lives blended well as we worked our way through the book. I couldn't have done this without her, and when I asked her to write the forward, she cried. It would be one of the final accomplishments of a long and fruitful life of service.

She passed shortly after emailing the foreword. Knowing what she faced, perhaps it was an unexpected mercy that our Father brought her home before we were ready to lose her, but I have yet to finish processing the loss.

As I wrote this, I cried.

The Baker and the Bread
And
The Forgotten Ones Crusade

On May 9th, 2018, I began writing The Baker: Prelude to a New Kind of Life. I had not written much since college but obeyed the Lord's command to tell my story. After completing the book, I haphazardly stumbled into blogging online through The Baker and the Bread on Facebook.

The book sold enough, but the blog took off immediately. From not writing much more than a few letters in my life to prolific publication, Grammarly recently notified me that since 2019, it has analyzed more than 18,000,000 words. I must enjoy it! It has borne fruit as a ministry, reaching millions in over seventy countries and over fifty languages. It became one of the most active and engaging pages in the world when, suddenly, it was mysteriously "hacked." Somehow, Facebook couldn't figure out how to give me the page back.

My admin team and I stepped back, adjusted, and diversified. The Baker and the Bread is now The New Baker and the Bread. At the time of this writing, with only 3,000 followers, we're reaching over half a million people a month. God's Word will not be quenched, and social media has led to our next move and God's calling: the Forgotten Ones Crusade.

The homeless population in our country on any given day is nearing six hundred thousand; 1.2 million are in prison, tens of thousands reenter society through halfway houses, while drug addiction soars and national overdose deaths surpassed one hundred thousand last year. Another 1.2 million elderly are shut away in nursing homes, 3.5 million teens are on the streets, and over half a million are without guardians. Partnering with local churches and ministries, The Forgotten Ones Crusade is designed to reach these. While working with the local Body, most of my time will be spent in the streets, alleys, beneath bridges, in halfway houses, shelters, and nursing homes – wherever they are. I will hopefully be joined by those called to such a purpose. Teams are already preparing for this in many places, and I am working with them.

The Forgotten Ones Crusade will take me on the road for 4+ years on a missionary journey across the country. At this point, I'm scheduled to go to 160 cities, and I may add more.

Like one of the New Baker and the Bread's on Facebook, the focus is to remember those society has or would rather forget, those our Lord has never forgotten. The homeless, disenfranchised, and disconnected; the addict and alcoholic; the prisoner and ex-con; the elderly in nursing homes or homebound; and dispossessed children and teens.

I will engage with local churches and ministries. I will speak at many and lead seminars to help them establish a ministry or bolster their current ones. I've had a good amount of success where I am, and I have a platform that regularly reaches millions to encourage Christians far and wide toward service and to share the journey.

This is my calling and my passion. God has purposed me for this, and with God's calling, an online team, and boots on the ground, I hope to work diligently in the fields of harvest.

The numbers above are immense, and that presents a perception problem. We often make the mistake of viewing people in groups and feeling successful when we feed large numbers or shelter many, but that begs the question of why we are doing it. We get lost in the numbers and judge our success based on them, creating a disconnect in our minds. Ministries often feed the body but leave the spirit to languish. Conversely, churches will succor the spirit and leave stomachs to rumble in despair, bodies shiver in the cold, and minds are left to the wasteland of mental illness. We sometimes forget because we only see the numbers and try to tackle them instead of the root of the problem – the individual.

It's difficult to tell a hungry man about the bread of life, and a mind plagued by mental illness has difficulty grasping the Hope of Christ. If we only address the body and mind, we perpetuate the sickness of society that has reached epidemic proportions. After all, the heart of the problem is a problem of the heart. We must find ways to navigate past the physical and psychological to reach the spirit, and that can only happen one way. We can solve societal ills like homelessness, but it will be done one relationship at a time.

The Forgotten Ones Crusade is just this: it is a call and an effort to return to our roots that Jesus first planted – relationship evangelism. He met the fishermen by the seashore, Matthew at the tax collector's table, and the demoniac of the Gadarenes in the graveyard and called them in a way they could understand. He met them where they were, as they were, called them to be with Him and on to service.

If you have further questions, please reach out, and I hope you'll join me for the Forgotten Ones Crusade.My contact information is below.

In Christ Alone,
David Riordan

857-287-4041
Info@thebakerandtheBread.com
The New Baker and the Bread on Facebook
The Baker and the Bread @DavidRiordan215 on X
The Baker and the Bread @thebakeradthebread428 on YouTube
The Baker and the Bread on Instagram
TheBakerandandtheBread.com

Introduction

This is my life. It happened. While anyone would
desire the end, and there were great things at the start,
I have changed most of the names and locations
to protect the guilty because no one
would willingly choose my

Beginnings

BOOK ONE

WHO I WAS

OR

OH MY,
WHAT A DISASTER

OR

COULD ANYBODY
REALLY SCREW UP
THAT BAD

April 10, 2018

I have no doubt my life is in danger, and I am confused and overwhelmed, but I know I have no real friends in the drug world. They have stolen or destroyed everything I own. They have taken over my father's house. Thinking they were projects of mine, my father invited one of them to live in the spare bedroom and work for her room and board. I wish he had asked me first.

Of course, I should be able to call one of my control officers, but I do not know who I can trust. One thing is for sure: they made many promises and have delivered on none.

I have 24 hours to get out of town. I have had multiple attempts on my life. I live under threat. I am no dummy. If my life is in danger, I am protected from prosecution if I must break the law to preserve life.

I can no longer trust those who wear badges; they have failed me, and I need somewhere safe.

I will take the advice I gave my best friend's son and drive west until the wheels get wet. My car has been stolen; I have no vehicle, so I will rely on my father's grace.

Because I leave tonight, I must leave this record so someone will know. I will borrow my dad's R.V. long enough to get to safety.

I pray the Lord protects me. I do not deserve it. I started this for all the right reasons. I have screwed it up—not by lying or being dishonest with my handlers. It became too big for me, and we started with two different motivations. I don't know how I ever thought this could end well. And quite honestly, law enforcement has left me hanging out to dry.

1

How It All Began

"In the beginning, God created...."

I'm kidding. In January 1965, Jerry and Betty Riordan were expecting their fourth child. So naturally, a heightened sense of expectation filled the house. Already the parents of three healthy children, Danny, age six; Becky, four; and Timmy, two—excitement grew, for they would soon have a complete, perfect American family of two boys and two girls.

They chose potential names and pulled Becky's baby clothes from storage in the attic of the Marietta, Georgia, semi-rural home where they lived. Mom, Betty, was prepared. They were ready at a moment's notice because she was not one to have any labor issues. With their first girl, Rebecca, Mom barely made it to the hospital and almost gave birth alone in a room because the nurse walked out to see if the doctor had arrived yet. She had packed her bags.

Dad, Jerry, planned as well. No delays in getting the love of his life to the hospital must happen. An up-and-coming, promising co-manager of a Kroger grocery store, he stayed near the phone as the February due date got closer. While far from wealthy, God blessed his little family. They lived paycheck-to-paycheck and moved to a less expensive home by about $15 a month to survive, but they were all content and healthy. Thoughts of another girl-child completed their view of a perfect home.

As you can already tell, I upset the apple cart, so to speak, from the beginning.

February 15, 1965, rolled around, and Mom's labor began at about midnight. But, by 2:08 a.m., her image of perfection had been shattered because, at 2:07, Dr. P.E. Parker announced, "It's a boy."

My mother's initial response was she was happy I was well. Nothing else mattered. It would be a few minutes before those emotions flooded through my father because in Georgia, at that time, fathers were not only discouraged from being in the delivery room, they were barred. The definite issue was putting the girl's clothes back up and finding a name for this child, which was important.

Day three of my nameless life progressed fine for me because, at that point, I didn't care. The change-the-diaper, reload-the-belly, change-the-diaper cycle was all that gave me any rise in concern. Then, as Mom dutifully and lovingly tended to those incessant demands from yours truly, my mother's nurse strolled into the room.

"Now, Mrs. Riordan, this baby needs a name!"

"Everybody told me it would be a girl. I carried him like I did my daughter. I have only thought about a girl's name," declared my mother. "I already have two boys. I didn't want another stinkin' boy," she smiled at the nurse with a twinkle in her eyes. "I just can't think of a good one."

"Maybe I can help," offered the nurse.

Mom stated firmly, "It has to be in the Bible for the first name."

The nurse gently took me from my mother's arms. "This looks like a little David."

With one fell swoop by a nurse who never saw me again, she entrusted me with the name mentioned in the Bible more times than any other—other than Jesus. He was awesome. As a young man, he killed Goliath with only a sling. He exhibited great spiritual ethos by not raising his hand against God's chosen king, Saul. He, for Heaven's sake (literally), designed and collected material for the Temple in Jerusalem. He was a hero.

He was also an adulterer and a murderer—a man so tainted with bloodshed the Lord forbade him to have anything to do with building the Temple.

In the end, though, he was a man who pursued having a heart like God's. He was a man who knew how to say, "I'm wrong; please forgive me." By being an example of a penitent, he became the ancestor of the One who brought true forgiveness.

"Not fair! Why saddle me with a name with so much baggage and responsibility?" Besides, I can think of better-fitting, more suited names for the man who has lived my life—Judas, who betrayed Jesus; Benedict Arnold, who betrayed his country through a mixed-up sense of moral priorities; indeed, even Adam, who betrayed all humanity. Those names fit me far better—certainly not in human magnitude, but then again, let's face it: on February 18, 1965, I had been burdened with the name of the man who established a kingdom that has no end. Wow! Or should I say, "Ouch!"

****

"You are such a smart young man!" If I heard it once, I heard it a thousand times. Exceptional genes were harnessed by parents who believed strongly in the one thing neither had for themselves—an education. So, they enrolled me in the University of Life at a very young age.

"University" is an interesting word. It was coined by diametrically opposed words—unity and diversity. The concept—now lost in today's institutions of higher learning—was that studying many diverse subjects could be utilized efficiently and proficiently only if theology unified them. It makes perfect sense. We can understand the diversity of all sorts of things if we study the One who made them.

My mom loved to tell the story of my first memorized Bible verse. Mom would teach my siblings a passage every week at the dinner table. She would start on Sunday night by saying the current selection, explaining it, and having them repeat it. She replicated this every night and allowed them to try it independently if they wished. My siblings usually memorized it by the end of each week.

Up to this point, I was not a participant in this ritual, for I was only two. I was simply a passive toddler at the dinner table. (Well, knowing me, I doubt passive ever described me.)

The verse in question was Isaiah 53:6--"All we like sheep have gone astray. We have turned every one to his own way, and the Lord hath laid on him the iniquity of us all."

Monday night—first chance—no volunteers.

Tuesday night — "Anyone want to try out the verse?" No volunteers until Mom started to leave the subject.

"I want to," piped up my little voice. (Again, knowing me, I doubt my voice was ever little.)

Mom, never to discourage the young ones in her charge, politely told me to give it a shot—to humor me.

I wasn't entirely out of diapers.

"All we, like sheep, have gone astray. We have turned every one to his own way, and the Lord hath laid on him the iniquity of us all. Isaiah 53:6."

Mom was nearly speechless. I did not have the vocabulary for this, nor a good sense of grammatical construction, yet I quoted it without error.

"And what does iniquity mean?" trying to recover from the complete shock.

"Bad things we do."

The shock was now complete—the dysfunctional starting gun sounded. "And he's off!"

I learned three things that night. One—it was possible to impress somebody by doing something out of the ordinary. Two—if I used my brain, it was easier to do one. And, three—I found great pleasure in doing that very thing!

In the attempt to be accepted by others, we develop behaviors that lead to gaining the respect and admiration of people around us. Reinforcement of those behaviors comes in many forms. Of course, praise from a parent and awe from siblings top the list. But I had achieved more than that. I had gone beyond simple expectations.

Much like a crack cocaine addict constantly chasing the initial high, I would spend much of my life trying to acquire those feelings again, though I do not remember that night in detail now.

The seed of dysfunction was planted that night because the event skewed my perceptions by the need to perform something unusual—overcoming what was, obviously to me, a weakness—being the youngest.

It is challenging for adults when they do not know how to deal with an abnormal child—especially when the abnormality appears positive.

And what is normal? It is an average, and nobody is one hundred percent average. Therefore, not being normal is the norm.

Dysfunction is, of course, harmful. It drove me to consume knowledge at a breakneck speed at the expense of gaining social skills.

I learned to read at three and was better read than most adults when I entered school. I had read, cover to cover, all twenty-two volumes of the World Book Encyclopedia. (For my younger audience, encyclopedias are sets of bound books that describe pretty close to everything and everybody important from A to Z.)

Did I understand it all at that age? Absolutely not, but I was building a knowledge base. With scripture memorization, I created a memory tool for everything—not just scripture. I had the kind of mind that perhaps I could have done something worthwhile.

In fifth grade, I scored above 12th grade across the board on all subjects on the ITBS (The Iowa Test of Basic Skills—a national standardized test).

I wrote so well during my school career that teachers accused me of plagiarism three times, and I was later vindicated. One of those times, in ninth grade, was for an 80-page term paper comparing and contrasting the governments of Iran before and after the Islamic Revolution of 1978-1979. The teacher had made a mistake she never made again—minimum requirements with no limit on the length.

I, however, was growing up in the shadow of giants. My siblings were and are so awesome. I would never be as good as them.

By the time I was old enough to know him, my oldest brother, Dan, was, in my mind, a rock star. Dan is the quintessential musical genius. It is undeniable. Now? He writes musicals for the church, where he is the music director. He can play any instrument. He is amazing. Back then? He played guitar in a Christian rock band—he was cool! But being the humble guy he is, he would deny the cool part. I still think he rocks.

Then there was Rebecca or Becky when we were younger. She had it all. She was (and is) beautiful with brains, talent, and a dynamic personality. She was a winner! She achieved "Governor's Honors" in English in high school and graduated early with honors. These are a few things from a long list of accomplishments during her teen years. But what would dazzle you is if you could hear her play the piano. She is one of the truly talented ones—technical brilliance combined with a passionate translation of the emotion behind the music—a concert pianist if she had wanted.

Finally, I have my brother, Tim. (Tim dropped the Timmy young, underscoring his good sense). Tim was the closest in age to me and the one I idolized the most. We both played football—he was a quarterback, and I played line. He was a star—until he realized he was not Doug Flutie. (They both stopped growing at 5'10). However, it didn't matter what he did; he was that guy—the one everybody liked and wanted to be. That's what was in my field of vision. Like my sister, he had the looks, brains, and talent. But after he graduated from the University of Georgia, the UGA Concert Choir "lost the best tenor it's ever had," according to the nationally respected choral director at the school. I know because I heard it with my own ears.

My insecurities did not need help, but they got it. By eleventh grade, if I heard it once, I heard it a hundred times, "Why can't you be like your brothers and sister? The funny thing is Dan will admit to a rather lackluster high school performance; however, by the time I got there, his musical accomplishments had overwhelmed people, so he got grouped with Becky and Tim, leaving me outside the box.

When I was 9, they were 12, 14, and 16. We were camping. I told them bamboo would sound like firecrackers if you threw it on a fire. The triumvirate responded in chorus to the negative.

To their credit, we all went and cut some bamboo down, threw it on the fire, and proved—for the first time in my memory—that I knew something they did not. However, I wish I had had better insight into it. Despite achieving the one thing I sought, an equal place amongst my siblings, I continued to have an underwhelming opinion of myself with an overwhelming compulsion to rise to their level. In my mind, I would never be as bright as they were.

Dysfunction grew. I had to catch up with my siblings! That's all there was to it. I began getting reading lists from their classes and grabbed their textbooks when they left them around. I became a consumer of knowledge but felt like catching up was impossible. I only wanted to be accepted. Every kid does.

However, reaching acceptance at 10 or 12 is hard when everyone thinks you're condescendingly using $100 words in a 20-cent economy. I did not know any better. I wanted to measure up. My target moved further away and was unreachable, but nothing else mattered. The more insecurities I had, the more I would try to learn. The more I learned, the less I fit in. The less I fit in, the more insecure I felt. It was a vicious cycle. I was doing a good thing learning, but the more I learned, the more distant I became from the one thing every child craves—acceptance.

In sixth grade, my teacher belittled me to the class as "weird" and "abnormal" because my vocabulary was more extensive than hers. They laughed at my expense while I was out of the room. The other kids were quick to tell me. Years later, I found out my mother went to the school and "tore her a new one"—if you know what I mean; however, Mom would never have told me at the time because she felt that would be disrespectful to the person of authority—the teacher. Respecting those in control over us was a big thing. Looking back, I could have learned another lesson. Learning to deal with someone effectively and respectfully in authority when they are wrong is a skill sorely lacking in today's world. I could have discovered so much more if my teacher and parent had come together and worked to solve an issue—not a bad issue—my educational level. That would have been the right thing, but the teacher's insecurity, my mother's Momma-bear knee-jerk response, and my lack of knowledge about the encounter left me where? (Lest anyone think for a moment I am unjustly on my mother's case—if my mom had been born 2000 years ago and been a Jewess, God might have overlooked Mary). At any rate, my dysfunction grew after missing the opportunity to learn something I didn't already know.

High school? I hardly went. I found every excuse in the world not to go. I made good enough grades, only showing up for tests. Why go? While it is true, for the most part, I knew what the teachers were teaching, I did not realize I was missing what the classroom taught. I needed to catch specific socialization skills. I missed learning to value others' input, often substantive yet not easily discerned by the uninitiated, even when you know the facts.

A reckoning would come for tangible lessons not acquired by skipping class. A funny illustration: as mentioned earlier, I had many words in my usable vocabulary—usable so long as I was writing. However, I hadn't learned specific pronunciation rules. I often used words perfectly in context but massacred the pronunciation. For example, I missed the pronunciation rule for terms longer than two syllables ending in a suffix—accenting the syllable in front of the suffix. I learned that at 32 from my wife at the time—e.g., syllabic = se-'la-bik.

I was a kid. I was way past confident to the point of being cocky. For those who might have had the patience to guide me, they'd have to look up the words in my arsenal before they responded, so most didn't. I soon learned that if I was going to do anything, it had to be by myself. With teenage angst and juvenile rebellion, you've got a recipe for what? A serial killer? An anti-social hermit? A mad scientist? A drug addict?

Well, a serial killer wouldn't work for me. I, with some frequency, would find injured animals and bring them home. I don't know if I ever healed them, but I sure tried! Broken wing on a bird? Popsicle stick splint. A baby bird fell out of a nest? To keep it warm, I made a "nest" in a shoebox, complete with a lightbulb. Sick dog? Fed, watered, and comforted. We now know torturing and killing small animals is a prelude to being a serial killer. I clearly failed at the introductory level.

The one time I found one beyond anyone's help, I euthanized it. It destroyed me for days. I could never have done that again!

Anti-social hermit? It might happen now. One of my favorite fantasies is living in a house in the mountains where my nearest neighbor is five hundred miles away. As a child? Being a "Riordan" meant being in the middle of things. We were smart and did not hesitate to speak out. There's not a shy one among us. Perhaps my sister, whose nerves were somewhat of a handicap, was a bit introverted. Still, our parents expected that no amount of nerves would stop us. We were to push through any obstacle. Starring roles in elementary school plays and church musicals and winning at state-level competitions was our standard operating procedure. The option of a hermitage was reserved for vacations only—then it was back into the fray.

Mad Scientist?

This one. I may have done this one. What's cooler than inventing things that nobody else has thought of? I put a lot of creative juice into designing things—I still do. It's the "Mad" part with which I would have had trouble. Mad scientists are selfish and care for nothing for others. It's the whole serial killer thing again. I may have been a typical selfish child, but seeking to harm others was out of my purview. It angered me when bullies picked on other kids because they talked, walked funny, or didn't have the funds to afford decent clothes. I got in more than one tussle as a child, defending the outcast. Perhaps it was because I was also an outcast, but I didn't appreciate watching someone ill-equipped to protect themselves getting picked on. I did not hesitate to jump in and defend another. I was a bit of a crusader. Mad Scientist Crusader might fit in today's sociological paradigm, but not so much in the 1970s. Another option was gone!

Only one destiny lay in front of me.

A lot of people are confused about drug and alcohol addiction. Perhaps the confusion started during the Vietnam Conflict when the use of opioids as painkillers led to a steep rise in chemical dependency. Although chemical dependency often accompanies it and can be challenging to overcome, chemical dependency is not addiction.

What is an addict, and how does someone become an addict? I have often said, and with some evidence and a certain amount of authority, since I am an addict, being an addict is not something most choose.

Active addiction requires three things. First, scientists have proven there is a Genetic Marker, thus making it hereditary. I am not a purist in the great battle of psychiatry vs. psychology—nature vs. nurture. But, as in most things, extremism is not the way to go. It makes sense that addicts come from a family of addicts, and environmental pressures play a role as a child matures. Third, the two above things leave an addict with little choice but to pick an object of their addiction. Genetics, environment, and, finally, choice complete the making of an addict.

If you have not noticed, I didn't mention drugs or alcohol explicitly in the above paragraph because addiction rears its ugly head in so many ways.

Using an outlet like exercise would be healthy. Sounds good, right? One of my siblings took up running as a teenager. He loved to run. He started running 10k races and worked up to competing in marathons. The more he ran, the more he wanted to run to the point he exceeded 100 miles running most weeks and developed Achilles tendinitis, destroying his favorite past-time.

According to Psychology Today's website, "Addiction is a condition in which a person engages in the use of a substance or in a behavior for which the rewarding effects provide a compelling incentive to repeatedly pursue the behavior despite detrimental consequences."

Addiction is symptomatic in other ways, but the addict, and sometimes society, find a way to justify their behavior. The workaholic becomes a "good provider," though his children are left to fend for themselves regarding social maturity. One of the most popular justifications comes from those suffering from the deadliest and most societally destructive addictions—food, "I may be overweight, but at least I don't do heroin/cocaine/etc." According to articles I have read, obesity has reached epidemic proportions, and the drain on the healthcare system and deaths related to being overweight are unmanageably high in the U.S. and most industrialized nations.

The fundamental handicap for an addict, in my experience, is the inability to deal with personal emotional pain. We addicts tend to bury the pain deep inside—not knowing how to process it effectively. Then, we resort to covering over the pain or hiding it with a substance or an activity.

With the other three options removed, my likelihood of acting on my addictive personality disorder became great.

Though behavior patterns entrenched themselves by the time I entered college, it would be a few years before substances became an issue.

April 10—11:00 p.m.

Dad is asleep. I have written a letter to him. I have explained I only borrowed the R.V. for a short time. Can I find somewhere safe? In the letter, I explained the necessity to him. I have no options left.

I have also told him in the letter that I will return the R.V. once I have repaired it. I have every intention of paying the credit card bill. However, I cannot start over again without the tools. My tools, down to my last screwdriver, were stolen by the meth addicts I have accumulated around me while trying to end the meth trade in Spelding County.

I have got to load everything I have left. The clock is ticking. I only have a little time left.

I just handed the letter to Ron to give to Dad. He helped me set up the battery charger on the R.V., so it will be ready to go as soon as I get whatever I have left to my name loaded.

I wonder if I can trust Ron. He is part of the crowd but has vehemently disagreed with them lately. So, for that reason and because I cannot delay, I have to trust he will deliver the letter.

2

Ingredients

After graduating from Griffin High School early, I began my post-secondary career at the University of Georgia. Go Dawgs!! My family had urged me to start at a nearby junior college. However, it was me! I had the highest S.A.T. score of anyone in the family, and I had taken that standardized test in the 9th grade. I was dead set on leaving everything in Griffin behind. I was going to conquer the world. They only needed to stand back and watch.

College was too easy, or so I thought; I breezed through the first couple of quarters, proving what I knew to be true. I aced my first few classes. I am the only person I know who went to U.G.A. then who managed to not only pass my first English essay in Eng. 101; I made an A. Even my Governor's Honors in English sister had not managed to do that. I got through the class with no problem.

My mother needed a lifeguard at the Flint River Baptist Camp, of which she was the Director. She needed a lifeguard trainer, so in my first quarter at U.G.A., I became a Red Cross-certified W.S.I. or Water Safety Instructor. I was now officially licensed to train lifeguards. I would work as a lifeguard for the next two summers and train the camp's other lifesavers. Life was a breeze, and all was well!

Little did I know I would have my first reality check and two significant emotional hurdles the following year.

First came the reality check. While it sounds great to be so bright that you can skip school and still score well enough to enter a major university as a freshman, as I have mentioned, I missed things.

One thing I chose to blame on teachers and ignore the facts was how I dealt with abstract math. It had now been three years since I had had any math, and I aced my last class in high school—Geometry. There's more to this story, though. I had a gap in my intelligence dealing with abstract math. I had already begun developing a pattern:

- Take a class.
- Struggle to the point of failing.
- Drop it before it damaged my G.P.A.
- Retake the course.

It worked for geometry, and I aced it the second time around. In my first year of college, I had to do the same with Calculus, and Probability and Statistics. While I can still do pretty complex equations in my head, I need help wrapping my brain around abstract math.

One of my biggest issues was I needed to learn how to study, and I had never had to work hard to attain knowledge. That inability to approach learning systematically would have a negative payoff in relationships. People are far more complicated than the subjects I studied and are not quite as easily classified. I was too quick to arrive at conclusions about people, and the sheer amount of vacillation in all of us denies rapid interpretation of an individual's behavior. I could discuss personality types ad infinitum. I had everyone pegged. I just had them pegged in the wrong spots.

The above made me ultra-sensitive where I was concerned and not sensitive enough where others were.

One of the crushing emotional events during my freshman year was my grandfather's death—my mother's dad.

We never spent much time with my mother's side of the family. They all lived in south Florida, 8-9 hours away. My dad's side of the family was typically 1 to 1½ hours away in Chattanooga, Tennessee. We saw them several times a year.

Grandfather, Mom's dad, was a professional fisherman and shrimper out of Fort Myers, Florida. When I was about twelve or thirteen, he had invited me to spend the summer on his boats. Mom told me I would have to wait until I was 16.

I was so excited at the prospect that I took magazine subscriptions to sailing and oceanographic magazines. I romanced to the nth degree how great it would be for two or three years until the year before I was to go when he developed cataracts, had eye surgery, sold his fleet, and bought a ranch, thus dashing my summer dreams for my 16th year. By then, my grandfather was larger than life in my mind.

Flash forward to my first year of college. I was sharing a trailer with my older brother, Tim. I came home from school one afternoon to find a note on the trailer door from Tim. "Grandfather died. I couldn't wait for you. Gone to the funeral." Talk about alienation! I wasn't worth an hour of his time to wait, and my feelings were of no consequence! Calling him was not an option because cell phones did not exist in 1983.

Then Jeanette Bram entered the picture. She was Tim's accompanist. Tim was a music major, and voice was his instrument. Jeanette was a piano performance major. She paid attention to me, and by the following summer, she was pregnant, and we got married.

The battle to marry was hard fought! When I found out she was pregnant, her father already had an abortion scheduled. Mr. Bram was a sales manager, and I told people I was a better salesman because I talked her into marrying me. The truth is, I clearly remember the very first of many occasions I now call "God Appointments."

Jeanette had decided to have an abortion. I talked her into coming to the mall with me. I talked a blue streak, to no avail. As we walked towards the mall's exit, a man approached, stopped us, and said, "God told me to come to the mall to pray for you." He prayed, and we left the mall engaged.

While the marriage eventually failed, I had two beautiful girls while still in college. You cannot make good relationship decisions outside of God's will. Of course, I wanted what I wanted when I wanted it, and whatever it was, I wanted it now. One decision—being with someone outside God's will, cost me untold grief, not only for myself but for her, our children, and our families. That pain has never stopped. No one wants to accept the responsibility for colossal bad decisions, so for years, since I made myself such an easy target, I have been used as a target practice for bad behavior. Whether justified or not, those using me for target practice—to cover their own inadequacies—have never had to face their demons. "At least I'm not like that sinner over there!" Jesus told the story of the Publican and the Pharisee praying. We all pull a Pharisaical move now and then. We all find easy targets. It is easier to accept ourselves if we have someone with whom we can look down our noses. That evil I initiated has continued through the years with drastic negative impacts, even on my three youngest children.

I was motivated and found that I could accomplish much by sheer force of will. While at the University of Georgia, I founded a group, "Christians Alive," for ministry. We sponsored a Creation vs. Evolution debate on campus. Between the months of discussion in the college newspaper and classrooms, lecturing opportunities to science classes, and the live debate, this venture was hugely successful with a large crowd and a decisive win for the creation side. How many 19-year-olds are given unfettered access to science classrooms on a major university campus? Of course, with each opportunity, each professor, except for one, had one goal—to show me up for the idiot I was. They failed.

My information was solid, my presentation tight, my debate skills, without any competition, and my force of will—all added to my success. But something was wrong. Ultimately, all the money I needed to round up never came in. The event, while excellent, left me empty at the end and with a financial hole I never bothered with. A lot of things in my life have gone through the same pattern. The force of will from a motivated, intelligent person can win many battles—but never the war. With each success/failure, I ventured further down the road to isolation. To me, the problem was obvious. God had given me talent—other people couldn't keep up; the failure was not mine, but deep inside, I always knew it was. I didn't know why.

In my isolation, I lost the sharpening effect of other people. Again, my excuse was others could not keep up, so I began to develop two sides of myself. One, the public personae, and two, the person others did not understand—the dichotomy of mind—singleness of spirit. I was not doing things for God. I was doing good things for myself—making a connection, catching up with my siblings, being valuable, and feeling loved. Nothing worked.

The separation from reality that existed—a dichotomous mind—led to my breakdown and resulted in me breaking the law and spending almost four years in prison.

The two most valuable lessons I learned in prison would bring great success and greater sorrow.

The first important lesson I learned was I was speaking a different language as far as others were concerned.

I mentioned my rather large vocabulary earlier. On a high school vocabulary test, my usable vocabulary was roughly twice the size of a person with a Ph.D. I never realized a significant communication gap between myself and others existed.

A learning moment for me was when a fellow inmate looked at me and said, “You know? Nobody understands anything you say. Why don’t you dumb down for the rest of us? People may like you better.” By the time I was paroled, I had not only learned how to communicate with different people on different levels but also gained my wonderful Southern drawl, for which my friends now know me.

The second lesson I learned was that, like it or not, and fair or not, a choice might define you for the rest of your life. I was a convict. In many ways, the life I wanted to have was over. Chances of getting a “good” job were over. Others would not accept me on an even playing field.

Upon my release, I felt the stigma of being an ex-con in every facet of life—including in the church. While not always true, people did look down their noses at me, and it both motivated me to excel despite what they believed and gave me an excuse to fail.

Jumping from disaster to disaster became my modus operandi. I could roll with the punches and force things through by sheer force of will. Thinking fast, I could always stay one step ahead of the consequences of each disaster.

I was motivated and intelligent, with the work ethic of a workaholic handed down honestly from my father. I gained skills and some success in construction. I became a go-to guy for some architects in Atlanta for the design and installation of metal roofs. I helped design roof systems for no-dollar-limit warranted roof systems for a couple of roofing manufacturers. The chief engineer of one of the world's largest roofing manufacturers once told me there probably weren't ten people in the Eastern U.S. who understood roofing the way I did. I was somebody.

I should have felt some modicum of success. I should have felt like I belonged. I made money, but I needed more. Acceptance from the ones I considered most important never happened—my family. It did not matter how much I helped or how they helped me; I always felt a step lower than them. I would never measure up. The problem was that I held the measuring tape but measured the wrong things.

I gave up. It became better for me to be high than to live in the real world. Already, I had shuttered my business when it was about to explode with absolute success. I had gone to work as a "hired gun," so to speak. I became a salesman, project manager, and, once, a division manager for other companies. Yet, I was still considered a golden boy in the roofing industry.

After leaving a top-echelon roofing company, the owner once tried to slam me publicly and was laughed out of the room. My abilities spoke for themselves. I had that kind of public reputation.

The dichotomy of mind and singleness of spirit dominated my life. I had learned to cover that duplicity well. I craved something I did not have, and everything in me strove to fill the need. I had access to what I needed. I had accepted Christ as a child. The life-fulfilling power of Jesus was in my clutches. I refused to use it. I was like a starving man with a warehouse full of broccoli. (I have forever hated broccoli). I would rather starve to death than eat the broccoli.

The problem was I did not want to relinquish control. To take advantage of the fulfillment of life, I had to let God have the reins. I had heard it in church. As life went on, I heard it time and time again in A.A. meetings and rehabs in my many failed attempts at getting clean. I failed so many times because I thought I could do a better job running my life.

Even after 15 years of continuous cocaine use, I got clean only because I had to go into enforced rehab by the state of Georgia. No drug was worth being locked up. I am a fan of coming and going as I please. I "white knuckled" it. In other words, I wanted to get high, and the only path to staying clean was through sheer force of will that had done so much else for me. Ultimately, my best efforts left me walking in torrential down-pours down Georgia roads. Alas, I will get ahead of myself if I am not careful.

April 11—3:00 a.m.

The R.V. is loaded. The battery is charged. I have filled up the gas tank and am ready to go. My worst fears have been realized. When I left to get fuel for the R.V., a sheriff's deputy was sitting at the end of my street. He pulled me over. He did not seem the least concerned that drug deals were going on in my driveway. His only concern was I was leaving town.

My worst fears? They are that the people who were supposed to protect me were behind the attempts on my life. I am not a big conspiracy theorist, but it seems to be without question that, at the very least, they are allowing bad stuff to happen to me.

I cannot afford another attempt on my life. The next time might be successful. Back in January, I was "one good kick away from dead," according to the emergency room doctor. The case of my assault has never been "solved," yet it took me less than two hours after I was released from the hospital to find out the names of all five people who assaulted me. "Something is rotten in Denmark!!"

3

Measured

I had had success in life. I had earned more money than most people would in their entire life. I had gone from ex-con to well-respected in my industry but also lost a fortune and respect.

The greatest blessing I had ever been given? Unquestionably, it has to be my children.

My children represented the one chance to achieve what I had always missed: acceptance from my family. Building my own could be the answer if I could not get it from my birth family. But the ever-elusive happy family would, time after time, escape my grasp.

I had two children, Abigail and Lydia, while I was in college.

Then came three years of prison. Many would say my first wife had reason to leave me while I was locked up. Plenty told her to. While in substance, she did; she, like most people, preferred to keep their sins private. She also comes from a family where appearances are more important than fact. She waited until I was released before filing for divorce.

Her parents never understood why the divorce decree did not bury me. That is a lesson I should have learned from her in that situation. Public sin can be devastating, but private sin can also destroy you.

However, she has done her damage and enlisted the right help to do her worst.

There was always an issue with me picking up the girls for visitation. It took me two years of driving 120 miles to pick them up and being refused visitation every other weekend before I could drag her into court.

In the meantime, she had married the sheriff's son, Mick Marr, of her home county, which only exacerbated the issue. In addition, the sheriff had held that post as one of the longest-sitting sheriffs in Georgia history, providing him with much political clout, which he did not mind using.

To put things in perspective, not only was I being denied visitation, but Jeanette told the girls I never showed up and didn't pay child support. She also drilled it into their heads that I did not love them.

I fought the battle. It is good my name is David, for I was going up against Goliath.

When I filed the paperwork with the court, acting as my own attorney, I suddenly got a call from Jeanette. She would allow me to pick up the girls the following weekend.

It was my first brush with how brutally evil and sinister people can be. It put those I had shared prison with to shame.

I picked the girls up, and we had a great weekend. Sunday night rolled around. We hopped into my truck and headed back to Welsington, Georgia.

As we were getting out of the truck, unbeknownst to me, Eve accidentally hit the lock mechanism on the door. My daughter's mistake saved my hide.

As soon as my door closed, I realized what had happened. 12-year-old Eve spoke up. "It's okay; Mick has a slim Jim," Mick worked for his father at the sheriff's department. It would be a reasonable assumption.

Mick walked out the door, heard Eve's question, and reached inside his house to retrieve a radio. He spoke into the radio, and in under a minute, an undercover police car rolled into his driveway. Three rather large deputies piled out of the vehicle. None would meet my stare. One, with a rather sheepish look on his face, proceeded to unlock my truck door. Without saying a word, the three returned to their vehicle and disappeared into the night.

As I backed out of the driveway, what had happened suddenly became clear. The officers had been waiting for me to drop the girls off. Then what? As far as rumor is concerned, I would not have been the first innocent person locked up in that county.

A few weeks later, in court, as a coup de grâce to my case, I brought up the aforementioned Sunday night. I told the judge I had no idea what they had planned to do—maybe plant drugs on me—I didn't know. The judge looked Mick in the face and asked if my statement was true. To Mick's credit, he did not deny it. But, of course, he wouldn't admit to the wrong either. The judge ruled in my favor and told Mick that if he ever interfered with my visitation again, he would revoke Mick's peace officer's license in Georgia.

I won the day, but Mick and Jeanette Marr would exact their revenge as time passed. Right and wrong mattered not to these people—one with whom I shared six years and two children.

Life went on in and out of failed relationships. My insecurities hampered my ability to choose well. I am convinced now that even if I had managed to find the "right" one, the relationship would never have been successful, for I could not have been the right one for anyone.

A lot of men would love to find a Proverbs 31 wife. Let's face it; the woman discussed in the last chapter of Proverbs is a superwoman! She does it all. She cooks and cleans. She plants the crops and harvests them. She makes the clothes the family wears. She is the perfect woman. Included in the description of the ideal woman is wisdom.

Even a small amount of wisdom would have driven a woman away from the broken person I was. How funny is it that the average person in a failing relationship always points at the other person as the one to blame? The real question is, why do we choose the people we choose? If we are such wise and wonderful people, why do we pick broken others?

Why do some women suffer from Battered Woman Syndrome? It happens so often that there's a name for it. In new relationships, women who have formerly had abusive relationships often find themselves in the same situation. After exiting a relationship with an alcoholic or an addict, many find themselves right back in a relationship with an alcoholic or an addict. Etc. Etc. Etc.

A Proverbs 31 Woman implies a Proverbs 31 man exists. The Proverbs 31 man is wise, hard-working, and perfect in love for the Proverbs 31 Woman, which makes him attractive to the Proverbs 31 Woman.

Without question, I was not a Proverbs 31 man. Wise women would steer away from me, leaving me with women of questionable ability to choose a suitable mate—an equal to my inability to choose well. I could not see why, but toxic relationships were the only kind I was destined to have.

When I began to experience real financial success, the second of two toxic relationships ended. Relationships never ended well for me. I had too many insecurities, and a breakup would bring me down lower and lower each time.

As I began to climb out of the depression of the last breakup, my brother-in-law began to tell me about a secretary who worked in the executive offices with him at the Kroger Company in the regional office in Atlanta. Her name was Molly, and Steve never seemed to find the time to introduce me.

This opportunity had potential on several levels. First, I grew up in a Kroger family. Dad was a courtesy clerk or bagger when he met Mom, a cashier. When they married, she left Kroger, and Dad began to rise in the company. My parents' story is the most remarkable love story I have ever witnessed. Kroger treated Dad well and, by association, his family.

As a company, Kroger was inextricably intertwined with my parents' love story. The success of our family life and Dad's career were almost synonymous in my eyes. While growing up, we were not wealthy, per se, but we were comfortable. There was always food on our table. We had excellent health insurance. When Mom worked, it wasn't out of necessity. She worked to provide us kids with the extras in life—piano lessons, football, baseball, basketball, school trips, and Bible Memory Association participation. Dad's job with Kroger gave us security. Mom's work gave us life-building experiences. Without Kroger, nothing else would have been possible. We all knew this, and while we never really saw Dad except on vacations, Mom taught us to appreciate Kroger, and we did.

After moving multiple times and landing in Griffin, Georgia, somewhere along the line, Dad hired a high school student, Steve, as a courtesy clerk. Steve met my sister at church, and after finishing college at the UGA business school and entering the management training program, they married. He is business brilliant and rose through the ranks until he wound up in the executive offices of Kroger in Atlanta.

A sense of romance about Kroger was already present in my mind.

On May 17th, 1997, I walked into my sister and brother-in-law's house at the end of a workday. Steve said, "Change your clothes. Get ready. We're going to a concert." So I showered, threw on my white Tommy Hilfiger long-sleeve shirt, and borrowed a pair of jeans from him.

This was not an unusual thing. Because of his position with Kroger, Steve often got free tickets to concerts and sporting events. From seats behind home plate for the wild-card clinching last game of the Braves' last-to-first 1991 season to executive booth passes for game seven when they won their first pennant of the decade to concert backstage passes, my brother-in-law produced the best seats for me.

So, Steve got good tickets, and I was often the beneficiary. It was not unusual for him to say we were going out. We were halfway to Atlanta before he informed me it was to an "Oldies" music concert. I love all types of music, but the bubblegum rock of the '50s and '60s was way down on my list of preferences.

To assuage the obvious negative feelings he must have felt I had, he said, "There'll be plenty of girls." That succeeded.

For once, Steve did not have the best seats. They weren't even center stage. As we found our places, I saw a cute blonde several rows in front of us at center stage. "Hey, Steve. Check out the blonde in the blue shorts and pink shirt."

"That's the girl I've been telling you about. Molly."

"Never mind. I don't need you now," at which I began to contemplate the best line I could come up with. Finally, after an hour and a half, I settled on my best effort and found myself heading in her direction.

"Molly!" I yelled above the music, "You don't remember me, do you?" (I know it was a terrible line).

"No, should I?" she yelled, and I iced the cake with, "No, but you will."

That was 5-17-97. Seventeen days after our first date, I told her I loved her. We were set at table seventeen at a concert. We were married on 8-25, 17 if you subtract 8 from 25. We found 17s in so many places it became our number. We had our official wedding seventeen months from the day we met at Chateau Elan in Braselton, Georgia—even though we had been married for some time. It was the best party to which many had ever been. People idolized our relationship. Our picture still hangs at the entrance of our favorite hangout. We were what everybody else wanted to be.

I had arrived! I was successful. I had a relationship envied by everyone. I felt the romance! We had an official number, 17. It was everywhere we looked—including in the number of years we were to be married.

April 11—5:00 a.m.

I don't know where I am going. All I know is it will be a while before I can come back—if ever. I've determined I have to say goodbye to Paul and Grace. For all practical intents and purposes, life, bad choices, danger, and lies from my daughter have stolen them from me. Despite others' best attempts, I have a good relationship with them both. Paul has been aware of what I have been doing since the beginning. He has known the danger I have been in, and despite missing me, he will have some comfort in knowing I will be getting out of town safely. I cannot leave without saying goodbye. First, I need to go to Welsington to see them on my way out of state, so I have driven in the opposite direction I intend on going—west until my tires get wet in the Pacific.

I need to tell someone in authority what's going on, but, at the moment, I need to figure out who to go to. There's no one I trust in Griffin anymore.

I am almost out of gas already, and I have no money. I can beg for gas. I can handle this.

Paul and Grace will be up soon, and I am only 30 minutes away. Then I can handle getting some gas and figure everything else out.

4

Sifted

I had no experience with gateway substances. I had tried a toke of a joint once. It was a negative experience. I have a weird body chemistry. I hallucinate on pot, which is not a good hallucination experience for me. Others had introduced me to ecstasy and LSD in prison.

I should have been prepared. I had been raised to believe drugs were terrible. I had already discovered alcohol, but I did not like being drunk. I had seen the commercials, "This is your brain on drugs…."

I, however, was not and never had been comfortable in my own skin.

In January 1990, a three-year stint in prison ended. I was glad to be home, but I was an ex-con, a college dropout with no usable skills. However, I now had begun to master the art of communication. While I might miss some things, I understood what motivated people to buy.

People bought from someone they trusted, and people trusted someone they liked. I had a great understanding of what it took to sell something. I didn't realize that until the only job available was selling knives.

These weren't just knives; they were the best—CUTCO, and I believed in them. I began to make progress as a salesman. Within the first few months, I broke records for new salespeople. They promoted me to assistant manager. I trained salespeople. I taught the salesman who broke my records. I won trophies, honors, and the opportunity to open an office.

Famous last words, for me at least, "I met a girl." Lisa was hot! She was cool, drove a sports car, and had a crack cocaine habit. I had never heard of crack, and when she introduced me to it, I thought I'd give it a whirl.

Three months later, I was broke, lost my office, and jailed. I was now a two-time loser with a dreaded label — "drug addict."

I lost another year between jail and a short stay in a county work camp. I came out clean. All I had to do was "just say no," and I did—for a decade.

I had beat drugs. I wasn't an addict anymore. I would never be that stupid again. I was sure of it.

Only now, I needed a job again. I wasn't going to do the sales thing again. It was too easy, the money didn't seem fair, and I was embarrassed. I needed to do something else.

I needed to find a job. Finding a job required gas in the tank. True to form, my dad would help me up. He offered me 50 bucks to paint his front door. It sounded great until I discovered the frame, decorative posts, and lintel were all rotten.

I pulled the trigger on a circular saw and a few other tools for the first time and rebuilt the doorway from the inside out. I had a knack for it, too. As recently as a year ago, close to thirty years since, I went back by the old house. I did a fantastic job, and it would have been considered very good if I had any experience, but I had never put two boards together in my life!

I got more construction jobs. I bought books on building. I passed all inspections. I have never failed any inspection because I learned from books. I didn't take shortcuts.

I discovered roofing when I completed my first addition. After that, I moved to Florida, where I combined my sales ability with roofing and became a roofer. Then, I moved back to Georgia as a roofer with certifiable skills. I was competent.

Halfway through the 90s, I sat conversing with a contractor in a bar. When he discovered I was a roofer, he asked me a life-changing question, "I'm building a hotel down in Thomaston. How much should the labor be on a standing seam metal roof?" Not wanting to sound like an idiot, but I had no clue what "standing seam" even meant; I did some quick calculations—quadrupled the best shingle price and then doubled it. "If you can do it for that, I just lost my roofer, and you can have the job." I was suddenly terrified, but I am a risk-taker at heart, and I took the job.

It took me three months and going through laborers like they were a dime a dozen, but I had found my way into a good niche in the roofing business.

I learned fast, and within a very short time, I left the small-town Market of semi-rural Georgia for the more lucrative Market in Atlanta. I became a preferred roofer for some architects. I lent them my knowledge of various types of roofing applications, and they referred me to their contractors. It would be a few years later before I ever had to bid against another competitor to secure work. I had once again achieved a level of success few enjoy.

Then, I began to have some health difficulties. I found out I was diabetic and had my first heart scare. I concluded my business was destroying me, but I was an achiever. I had married Molly, and we had Miriam. I turned contracts worth millions in and put my resume into the Market. One of Georgia's oldest and most prestigious roofing companies quickly snatched me up.

Within six months, I had outsold all the other seven project managers combined twice at several times the profit margin. I was feeling my oats. I was somebody. I was proud. When the president and primary owner of the company broke his word to me, I didn't hesitate. I quit.

I didn't miss a step. Another company looking to start a sheet metal division snapped me up. As the sheet metal division manager, I hit the ground running and began to grow another unscrupulous man's business.

Every addict finds excuses for using. I am not exempt. The reasons are honest in most cases. The addict who finds his DOC (drug of choice) in opioids because he has been in an automobile accident justifies using a little more each time. After all, the pain is real. The alcoholic businessman needs to destress after too many long days at the office, and one drink every night will not hurt anybody—which slowly moves to two drinks and so forth.

In my case, I had a perfect storm brewing. Life had become more complicated. Molly, I, and 1-½-year-old Miriam had to manage our money. I made good money, but it was nothing like I had been making.

It had been feast and famine in my business, but it had been a feast in the previous couple of years.

One of the last jobs under my company's name was a multi-million dollar contract in Newnan, Georgia. The first 90 days on the job were famine. The General contractor withheld my draws for no good reason. I had 32 employees that I had to pay every week. By the 12th week, with a payroll exceeding $15,000/week, I was about to go under. The GC released all three months' draws on day 91.

The rest of the job went smoothly. Somewhere near the end of the job, a holiday weekend occurred, and we were up against a hard deadline. Rather than waste time letting my guys go to a bank and knowing I needed to solve payroll for them before the end of the day, I brought payroll checks and enough money to cash them to the job site.

After cashing everyone's checks, being in a rush as I typically was, I threw the extra cash in the glove box and forgot about it. I was driving my wife's car instead of my truck.

A few weeks went by, and an emergency happened. Molly's grandfather had passed away in Indiana. We hopped in her car and drove to Indiana. After the funeral, we headed back in the direction of Georgia. Blue lights ahead at a roadblock caused me no concern. I pulled up next to the state trooper and asked Molly to hand me the insurance card. As she opened the glove box, $1500 in twenties and ones erupted. I got more than an intriguing look from the trooper.

I hadn't missed the money because we didn't manage the money; I made more than we could spend—except when I didn't.

Molly was a stay-at-home mom with little to put her mind on—other than raising a compliant child. I am not making light of the Mom's job; Miriam was easy. It became her practice to meet me at the door every evening with a list of daily grievances. Usually, something was wrong with what I was doing. That wasn't a great idea. I had often told her to let me walk through the door and unwind before pouncing.

It would never happen, but far more than that was going on then, and the foundation of a happy home was beginning to crumble.

Things were going fine at work. They were going great, as far as my career was concerned. We began showing a profit from the sheet metal division almost immediately. However, the low-slope, or colloquially "flat-roof," side seemed to take a step backward with each step forward. So, I also began selling work for and managing his side of the business.

The owner? He was more interested in his extracurricular activities. He was involved with his church. He participated in mission trips. He was a pious-looking man to anyone on the outside. He didn't feel quite as strongly about the mission field within his own company, for his employees did not go to his church and thus were not as visible to the ones he was trying to impress.

Two things were to happen during that year that impacted me emotionally. The first would devastate many hearts and minds in America, while the second was closer to home.

On September 11, I walked into the office from an early morning job-site meeting with an architect and a General contractor. Again, I was riding the emotional wave of success. Things went well. I was a problem solver, and my solutions were well received.

As I walked back into our office, everyone was glued to a TV set, and before I could brag on my success, the secretary said, "A plane just crashed into the World Trade Center." Not too long before, a small plane had accidentally crashed into a skyscraper in New York City, so a repeat was what jumped into my mind. However, watching the screen dispelled the notion. As we continued to watch, we saw the second plane crash into the other tower, only to see both buildings crumble. I was dumbfounded.

I had another meeting an hour away in Atlanta. Listening to the non-stop coverage on the way to Atlanta, I heard the potential death total of more than 80,000. That number would have held if the terror attacks had happened an hour later.

It was mind-numbing. I had been in the Georgia-Pacific building in Atlanta, where approximately 40,000 work. My mind replayed the sights of all those I had seen suffering a similar fate. And that was only part of it, for building number 7 fell, the Pentagon, and a no longer empty field in Pennsylvania.

Not many of us who lived through 9/11/2001, witnessing what we did, made it without scars etched into our memories.

While the terror attacks on 9/11/2001 played havoc with my emotions, another event would have a far more profound impact on my life.

Meetings. Nothing happens without them. This particular one required the owner and me to be present. I was driving, and as we were heading down Highway 78, nearing the office, one of my three cell phones rang. Molly asked to speak to my boss. That was unusual, but I passed the phone over. He conversed for a moment and hung up.

"David, why don't you pull over." My mind quickly raced through what I thought were all the possibilities, from she was leaving me to something had happened to hers or my parents. Nothing I imagined would require me to pull over.

I looked at him, "Have you ever seen me panic?"

He contemplated briefly and shook his head, "Eve has been in an accident."

That was not one of the scenarios rolling through my mind. "Is she at the hospital in Welsington?" (40 miles from where Eve lived with her Mom).

"She's being life-flighted to Athens Regional."

Never one to panic, I drove him back to the office and went to pick up Molly from home, while inside, a part of me died.

We got to the hospital emergency room, only 5 miles from my home, before the helicopter landed. We waited. The ER was waiting for her arrival, as well. Twenty agonizing minutes passed by with no word. At 45 minutes into our wait, a nurse approached, "We don't know why, but they have taken your daughter to the hospital at the Medical College of Georgia in Augusta.

Frustrated but not one to lash out at someone beyond legitimate blame, I grabbed Molly's hand and rushed her back to my truck. It's at least a two-hour drive from Athens to Augusta, but we made it in less than one.

An important note for later: About halfway to Welsington, I noticed a mile-long stretch of road soaked from a recent storm. I even noted it because the sky was completely blue, without a cloud.

Eve was in surgery when we arrived. Despite my frustrations over the delay in getting to the hospital, I could have done nothing if I had made it any sooner.

The surgeon entered the waiting room. Eve sustained incredible internal injuries. When the seat belt threw her back into the seat, her spine acted like a knife and sliced through her spleen, several places through her intestines, one of her kidneys, and severing her small intestine from her stomach right at the duodenum. "Surgery was touch and go. She's a strong young lady, but you should thank the first responders for keeping her alive. She shouldn't have been able to make it here. She is critical, and we will have to wait. Once she gets out of the critical stage, the real issue will be necrosis of her internal organs, particularly the intestines. It is now simply a matter of waiting."

The surgeon spoke with a no-nonsense tone, giving away his years of experience dealing with such injuries. But, as it turned out, he was all that and more. He was the head of the trauma department at the college, and his specialty? Abdominal trauma, pioneering methods of reattaching the small intestines to the stomach in injuries like Eve's.

God was at work. This surgeon didn't work that particular shift. Most of his time was spent at the college itself. Nevertheless, he had serendipitously been scheduled one night that week—the night of Eve's wreck.

We were amazed as the story about the accident and subsequent rescue unraveled.

Eve earned her driver's license only two weeks earlier. Her mother had gotten her a car and permitted Eve to drive down a highway and a long dirt road several miles away. The road had recently been graded, leaving a linear pile of dirt and gravel along the road's edge. Eve made a classic beginner's error. She, going too fast, ran over the edge, overcompensated, and ran into a tree on the far side of the road.

The damage to the car was catastrophic. Pieces were scattered down the road for many yards, and she was pinned inside the ball of decimated metal, formerly a vehicle.

No one was around. Eve knew she was hurt; the closest person was half a mile down the road. Thinking quickly, she turned her radio up as loud as it would go.

It would be an hour-and-forty-five minutes before the person ½ mile away would investigate the sound of a radio and find my daughter's broken, bleeding, almost dead body.

Another interesting note: I was told as the wrecker crew picked up pieces of the car, they found the battery wholly separated from the car several yards removed. Regardless, the car in that shape playing anything is a miracle—much less playing it at top volume for 1-¾ hours, even where the battery is present, but the road crew recovered it fifty yards from the demolished vehicle.

Another miracle occurred as the paramedics attempted to cut her out of the car with the jaws of life. By 2001, most police agencies had begun to switch to cell phones rather than using the inconsistent repeating radio. Not so in Moore County. A nationally recognized, award-winning, out-of-state paramedic on his way home from a paramedic competition where he had won top honors was riding nearby on the highway with a scanner on. He found his way to the accident site.

Arriving as the firemen were about to lift Eve out of the wreckage, he stopped them. He recognized the signs of massive internal bleeding. He took charge and turned the ambulance around to pick up plasma from the hospital. He administered the IV, they lifted her from the car, and she died. She had been in a positional tourniquet, stopping her from bleeding out. The foresight to call for plasma saved her, and they resuscitated her.

Meanwhile, on a bright sunny day, an unpredicted freak storm with a severe wind shear blew up, lasting 15-20 minutes between Athens and Welsington, blocking the helicopter from transporting Eve to Athens Regional. Forced to make a snap judgment and knowing they were equidistant from Athens and Augusta, with a storm to think about, he chose to go to Augusta.

The ambulance driver chose to go to Augusta where, unbeknownst to him, the head of the trauma department was scheduled one evening that week—the evening in question—who specialized and pioneered in repairing the very injuries my daughter had sustained.

The radio, the storm, the happenstance paramedic, and the surgeon—some might call these coincidences, but, of course, they were "God Appointments."

April 11—6:30 a.m.

Frustration. I needed more gas to make it to Welsington. I ran out in the middle of the road. I am in the middle of nowhere. Thank God a local police officer stopped. He helped me with some gas. I tried to solve the issue of telling someone in authority what was happening. He was a former Georgia state trooper. I liked him. I trusted him. I told him what was going on. I informed him of the attempts on my life. I told him I had borrowed Dad's R.V. without asking but had left a note. I told him I did not think there would be a problem with that, but I was scared. Since I was headed to Welsington and knew Mick Marr, he didn't want to be involved, but I should let Mick understand what was happening. I told him it might not go well, considering Sheriff Marr's disposition towards me. However, I am running out of options.

5

Broken Eggs

I was standing at the edge of a precipice in my life. With a high-stress job, dishonest employer, deteriorating home life, and a catastrophic accident for one of my children, I had potential life-changing choices to make. A sense of impending doom settled in my mind.

I had options. I was smart. I was successful. While the flower of addiction had not yet fully bloomed again, the stalk was out of the ground. Though I was an addict, I was not using. My background should have pointed me in the right direction.

My parents gave me a Biblical foundation. Scripture memory had begun before I was out of diapers. We were at church every time the doors were open, and Mom and Dad set examples in their personal lives that, I daresay, most pastors could not duplicate in their own lives.

Mom's passion in life was teaching children about Jesus. Some of my earliest memories are of Backyard Bible Clubs. Mom would teach these small groups of children throughout the city. Our church didn't organize the clubs. They were something she implemented. A Bible story, a Bible verse to memorize, songs to sing, and a craft designed around the story's theme were typical. The groups would meet outside in a neighborhood one day a week. She would go to a different section of the city on other days of the week when she got off from her job as a secretary for the church. She always took me.

Mom was also the church's director and teacher for Girls in Action or G.A.s. In addition, she taught children's church. She was involved, and Dad supported her work without question. It was important work. It was her passion and her calling.

In this environment, I began to put two and two together. My reading comprehension level was many years above my age. Jesus was real. He died for our sins, so I needed to ask Him into my heart.

One Sunday night at church (I actually paid attention in the service), I heard the pastor's altar call and asked Mom if I could ask Jesus into my heart. Being the wise woman she was, she said to wait until we got home.

She did this for two reasons. First, this was not a decision one entered lightly. Secondly, I was only five, and while she knew I was bright, she would ensure I understood what I was doing.

As I have aged and burnt many brain cells through drug use, my memory of many childhood events has faded. However, that night remains crystal clear in my mind. Neither of my parents brought up the subject but waited for me to bring it back up. When I did later, Dad took the matter into his hands. I remember his illustration of faith. It is an anchoring vision in my mind.

"Faith is not saying you believe something. It is putting action behind what you believe," Dad said. "I can say I believe this chair will hold me, but I show it when I do this." My dad is a conservative guy—always has been. So I expected him to sit in the old black, cushioned, metal arm-rest chair. Instead, astonishingly, he leaped up onto the seat with both feet. I don't think I would have trusted the chair if I were him, but he did, and it held and proved the chair was worthy of that faith. "Just like this chair didn't let me down, Jesus will never let you down."

As the illustration began to sink in, we dropped to our knees, and unprompted, I asked Jesus to come into my heart in my own words.

That night began a process in my life. Though I have made colossal errors, God wove an unbreakable strand into the rope of my life. Jesus would use it repeatedly to reel me back to Him.

My parents were committed to the verse in Proverbs about raising a child "in the way he should go." While I may have felt, and to some extent, I was indeed misunderstood, it never stopped Mom and Dad from doing their best. Their top priorities were raising us to be healthy, educated, and spiritually wise.

There is only one good reason I learned to read before I was three. My mother read to me consistently, so I would learn to read for myself. She had me on her lap, reading to me before I could hold my head up. She would follow along with her finger underneath the words as she read. Before turning the page, she would point to the terms and the pictures that went with the words and talk about the page. When I began speaking, she would ask me to point to and describe the images. And after I took my first steps, she walked me into a library and unlocked the door to the world of knowledge at my disposal. Later, I would follow her example and do all the above for my children.

To my parents, no difference stood between the quest for knowledge and understanding and knowing God! Of course, neither of them could have told you who Johannes Kepler was, but they shared a sentiment with one of the greatest astrophysicists of all time—in studying and learning, the best we'd ever be able to do was to "think God's thoughts after Him."

Scripture memory continued throughout my childhood. What had begun around the dinner table with a verse a week evolved into Bible Memory Association or BMA.

Based on age, a specific number of thematically arranged verses were required for weekly memorization. As a teenager, I memorized 14 verses weekly, reciting them with up to two weekly mistakes to a partial listener. Oh, make no mistake about it; the listeners were partial—not to us, the reciters, but highly partial to the accuracy of the scripture. On the third mistake, it was, "Go back and study until you can get it right!"

We would receive a prize every two weeks for participation. However, the biggest reward was after completing a season of participation; we got the opportunity to "audition" to participate in BMA Camp in Cleveland, Georgia. (I call it an audition, for lack of a better term). Of course, our parents paid for the week of camp, but to be allowed to stay, we had to recite two weeks' worth of scripture memory with only two mistakes and with only two attempts. You were sent back home if you made a third mistake on the second attempt. I remember one young man was sent back to Ohio because he could not recite the required two lessons. That was one lesson I would never have to learn, although it was not as if I was always prepared. By the time I was old enough, 9, I had honed my memorization skills sufficiently to look over two weeks' worth of scripture and remember it well enough not to make more than two mistakes. Those skills would serve me well in life.

BMA camp was a mixture of fun and in-depth Bible study—classes in the morning and evening with about three hours of recreation in the afternoon. The classes were exegetical, and the weeks spent at BMA camp during those seven summers of my life taught me a tremendous amount of mostly Biblical theology. I was astute at separating man's thoughts from what the Bible said. I was not thought of well by a couple of instructors. My logical thought and early-forming debate techniques were difficult for them to overcome, and I didn't mind speaking up.

My spiritual education did not stop with Sunday School and BMA. Participating in the Bible Drill for several of my childhood years, I frequently won local and regional contests, winning at the state level in my final year of eligibility. However, this was not your typical Bible drill competition, where you had to find a book in the Bible and step forward. Nope, this was more complicated. Books, individual verses, verses answering topical questions, and factual questions were all fair game in this Bible free-for-all, timed event where being second did not count for anything except for a ticket home. Being good enough meant being able to find any verse in the Bible in a matter of one to two seconds. At three seconds, you were done. I thrived in the competition.

A lot of things in life are, by necessity, competitive. If we are not competing against another person, we are:

· Farmers racing against the coming winter to bring crops in;

· A roofer finishing a roof before the storm hits;

· A trauma surgeon fighting seconds to save life.

Competition in our youth strengthens us for what life may throw at us, and I was a competitor.

I learned the art of competition through things like the Bible Drill and played football, basketball, and baseball. I entered contests of many kinds. I received trophies for many endeavors.

I won a blue ribbon at the state level in an art contest in high school for an exquisite photo of a sunrise when the sky was green. It happens every day for about 1/1000 of a second. It was a fortuitous picture. A shot like that doesn't happen because you're good. It is impossible to plan. I once read an article where a professional photographer spent decades trying to capture the green flash. I did it by happenstance at Myrtle Beach, South Carolina, as a 15-year-old with only one roll of film and not trying.

I performed well in competitions. I had trophies from all sorts of endeavors. (This was back when you only got an award if you won). I was not the most coordinated nor agile athlete, but I played well and was a starter on championship football and basketball teams. I won at Bible Drill. I won writing contests. However, as I aged and had to tackle a new challenge, I found something requiring real effort.

My first experience performing solo in front of people came with piano lessons. The Christmas Recital and the Spring Recital were both requirements of my piano teacher. I was not eager to practice, and practice is what you must do in piano performance. Getting by Piano National Auditions every year was easy enough by practicing and cramming the week before. I would only be playing in front of one person. That was intimidating, but it did not hold a candle to performing in front of others. No amount of cramming would prepare me for playing in front of people. I "crashed and burned" during several recitals through the years I took piano lessons. I should have gotten a hint.

I aged out of the Youth Bible Drill and into the Better Speaker's Tournament. The competition is easy to explain. Weeks before the competition was to take place, Judges delivered a list of topics. We had to choose one, write a speech, and propound. This would be a slam dunk for me, for Lord knows, putting the words together was easy enough. (Think 80-page term paper). And ask anybody who knows me; I love to talk. The competition would be judged on my writing and how I delivered it, with a time limit involved and penalties if it were too short. No restarts were allowed. If you went too long, the judges truncated your speech with a buzzer and the proclamation, "Time!"

I wrote my first competitive speech in about thirty minutes. It was good. Mom asked if I needed help, and I replied, "No." She asked if I was sure and walked away, leaving me to my impending doom. Mom was no dummy. It's why she knew it was not going to go well. She also perceived I would only receive it if I recognized I needed help.

The day came. The participants from around the local Baptist association began delivering their speeches. My name was called. I did not even finish the address. I froze. I stumbled over the words. I failed miserably and was so glad the five-minute buzzer sounded. I looked for the nearest hole into which I could crawl.

I came in second. The speech was written excellently. If I had finished, I would have won. A judge was kind enough to note on my card the quality of the writing did not match the presentation, and he recommended that I do the work involved for the following year, and I would win. Truer words have never been spoken because I needed to put forth the effort. In my mind, I had won before I wrote the first word, and I did not do the work involved. With nerves from performing in front of a packed church, it was a disaster.

"Son, I offered," was all my Mom said. It was heartfelt when I said, "I'm sorry I disappointed you. I'm sorry if I embarrassed you." With a sidelong look as she drove us home, she said, "Almost everybody knows me. They all know I would never do anything close to that bad. My reputation was not harmed in the least. You're the one who took a beating, and it was rather soundly. I wouldn't admit to anyone you came in second. You might have to explain why you didn't win."

Wow, and ouch!! If you can't handle the truth, you should never have asked my Mom for her opinion. She'd give it unsought but be more diplomatic with you. Instead, she let me feel the failure and the sting of defeat.

I won area and regional the following year and placed second at state. Mom said on the way home, "You were excellent, and I can't wait to tell everyone about your second-place finish. You have no apologies to make. The girl who beat you beat you, but it was really close." My mother, honest to a fault and my biggest fan, was the person who never gave up on me.

The never giving up on me part is the reason Mom so desired my spiritual growth would one day reach maturity. Spiritual growth is double-faceted. It is one coin with two sides. 2 Peter 3:18 proclaims when we grow, it is "in grace and in the knowledge of our Lord and Savior Jesus Christ." I had the knowledge part down pat. That was the part my parents had control over the most, and they gave me every tool imaginable.

Just as my activities were varied and multi-directional—piano/ center position in football, Bible drill/ Basketball, church/the liberal arts—my studies were diversified.

When I took my first job at 13, I used some money for magazine subscriptions. I took three magazines as a teenager. One was a magazine about sailing. Though I had never been on a boat, I had high hopes of spending the summer with my grandfather on one of his commercial fishing/shrimping vessels. One was for a Biblical archaeology magazine. I loved history and began to develop a taste for apologetics. The third was for comic books, in particular, Spider-Man. I loved Spidey, but I had a boy crush, for lack of a better term, on Peter Parker. If you know the story, you'll understand. He was nerdy-cool and brilliant!

I also loved the sciences. Besides reading anything I got my hands on, including every page in my older siblings' science texts, I began reading books specific to logic, the scientific method, and books on evolution and special design/creation. If transitional change was how it happened, I was cool with it, but I had to know. If it was not true, I wanted to understand why so many proclaimed evolution's veracity.

I read my first systematic theology in middle school, and in high school, I purchased my first one. Berkhof's Systematic Theology is not for the faint of heart, but I had to know everything.

I also read the first part of the Vedas, the ancient Hindu scriptures, and part of the Koran. I could tell you the difference between the accepted Christian Bible and the Jehovah's Witness Bible and why it made a difference. I studied Mormonism. I learned the differences between the protestant denominations. I could tell you why I was a Baptist and didn't care.

Jesus is the Lord of all, no matter what you want to call yourself. I knew all these things.

I knew.

Famous last words of mine.

Back to the 2 Peter 3:18 passage, "But grow in grace and in the knowledge of our Lord and Savior Jesus Christ." I had the knowledge part down pat. I had asked Jesus into my heart. I knew Him but did not understand the growth in a relationship with Jesus. My dysfunction kicked in both the spiritual realm and the temporal.

It would be 48 more years after my salvation experience before I would come spiritually face-to-face with the One I had met in the spring of 1970 at five years old. That meeting would come with darkening skies, a loss of all but one hope, and a song of praise from my lips.

April 11—7:30 a.m.

I called Paul and Grace. Lydia would not allow them to see me and told them she would have me arrested. They told me the police were waiting on me. They can't lock me up if I commit no crime. I am in Welsington anyway. I have gone straight to the sheriff's department. Sheriff Mick Marr is not in. I got his cellphone number and tried to call him to no avail. How can I report my situation to law enforcement if everywhere I turn, something corrupt is going on or someone does not feel the need to get involved?

I am going to Lydia's. She may act like an idiot, but she is my daughter. Perhaps I can talk some sense into her. I at least have to attempt.

6

A Little Bit of This

Disaster loomed ever closer. I was quite the successful plate spinner. You know, the guy who stands spinning sticks, puts spinning plates on top of them, and manages not to let them fall? That was me. Distractions spell the end of the entire show. How many distractions could I handle while continuously adding more spinning plates to the trick of my life?

I needed more employees at work. The Sheet Metal Division I was in charge of had rapidly expanded. I had discovered where sheet metal installers were concerned; hiring experienced help was a non-starter. In 1990, the metal roofing industry nationwide was a 100 million-dollar-a-year business. By 2000, it would become a ten billion-dollar-a-year industry.

I had been a part of the growth. I had designed part of the details for the manufacturers' no-dollar-limit warranted roof systems. So, in a small way, I have been a contributor to successful installations all over the world. I had built a business independently, and now I was making another man's. So, it was a heady time for me.

Plenty of people were looking for jobs who claimed experience. They rarely worked out for the same reason low-slope roofers wouldn't. Bad habits die hard. How you treated the material was important. You could toss shingles or manhandle low-slope rolls of modified roofing without damaging them.

On the other hand, metal had to be handled with kid gloves. Dinging and scratching it impairs the installed product's overall performance and causes eventual roof failure. Metal is as much about clean aesthetics as about performance. If people didn't care about looks as much as longevity, they probably would not choose to install a metal roof.

At any rate, I preferred hiring the untrained. It was easier to train the inexperienced than it was to break old habits. But then, a thought occurred to me. Some people have learned the significance of learning from mistakes, and they are a ready source for employment and would enjoy a chance to prove they have learned.

I began interviews at the local diversion center. I hired four men looking for an opportunity after serving prison time. They appreciated the opportunity because finding a job in such a situation is challenging. I would fire one. Two would complete their time at the diversion center and return home to other cities. One wanted to stay in Athens upon his release.

Mike had done well. He exceeded my expectations in acquiring the requisite skills on the job. In addition, he was older, more mature, and had a fantastic attitude. He had me pick him up on Sunday mornings to attend church with us.

Mike had a problem. After several months of employment, his release date from the diversion center approached, and he had nowhere to go. I made him an offer.

It was not an unusual offer for my family. We had lived for six months in Indiana, where my wife had grown up after I had shut my business down while I put my resume out into the world. Before we left to move to Macon, Georgia, for my first corporate roofing job, we met Jesse.

Jesse was 20, originally from Florida, and stuck in an infrequently paying job in what would soon be a winter-bound Indiana. He had no electricity and slept in front of a gas oven every night to stay warm. I did not have to twist his arm to convince him to move south with us. Two years later, Jesse moved to Athens with us from Macon and became part of the family, a big brother to Miriam.

There had been several "Jesses" in our lives through the years—Jeri, Frederick, Jimmy, Jenny, and others—who would stay for short periods to get on their feet. Still, Jesse was with us for the longest and became dear to us.

On the other hand, Mike represented a destructive force I should have noted—if I had been clairvoyant. I wasn't.

Despite my brief trouble with addiction, I had never spent time with drug users. Because my personal experience was so short-lived, I was not quite prepared for the deviousness of addiction—neither Mike's nor mine.

Mike needed a parole address, and I offered to let him move in with us, and he accepted.

I can see it all now, hindsight being what it is.

Sin rarely jumps on you with all of its ugliness. No, it presents itself well and slithers into your life. But, once in your life, it grows into a monster, slowly consuming you from the inside out.

I love J. R. R. Tolkien's representation of sin in the Lord of the Rings trilogy. Bilbo stumbles onto the "ring of power." The ring is valuable. It seems pretty cool. It helps him. However, soon after finding it, he lies to hide his attachment to the ring. The reasons for the lies seem reasonable, but the deceptions only grow larger and larger. He thinks he owns the ring. It is his "precious." The more time he has it, the more it possesses him until the ring dominates his life.

In the end, Sméagol, Bilbo, and Bilbo's nephew, Frodo, in their turns with the ring, only relinquished their possession because it was taken from them, after which the power the ring once held over them haunted their minds. Sméagol dies in his attempt to repossess the ring. Bilbo's and Frodo's redemption only comes because they can retreat to a place controlled by the Creator, and the ring was removed from their lives through no active decision of their own.

Wow! I would say Tolkien had a grasp of what addiction is. The truth is all sin is like what we label addiction. It is insidious and robs us of our lives.

At any rate, Mike moved in and continued to perform well on the job. He contributed to the household. Fall turned into winter, and winter to spring. All was well.

One week, after working long hours and having difficulty getting going one morning, Mike offered a solution. If I mixed a little "crank" or homemade methamphetamine in my coffee, I would have an easier time moving. Not enough to be high, just enough to knock out the exhaustion. In my mind, rationalizing this was easy. Out popped a little baggy, and as if by magic, what the caffeine alone would not do, my souped-up coffee suddenly did.

It was awesome! This was different from cocaine. There was no "rush." I used it like one would use medicine. I used it once, and I was good. No real need to do it again—until a couple of weeks later, then a few days after, then every day. Then came the day I bought enough to get high.

Not long after, Mike brought home some coke. I used it. I couldn't get high. I didn't know then, but "crank" or methamphetamine was a jealous drug. It hogs all the neurotransmitter sites in the brain cocaine uses. However, I was shocked I had tried it. I stopped everything. I wasn't going back down that road again.

A few weeks passed by. Then, things at work began to crash. Paychecks bounced. The owner had gone on a mission trip. Before leaving, he had emptied the company checking accounts. I scrambled and went on a collection spree of every customer who owed the company a dollar or two. I had done similarly for myself in the past. I knew how to coax money from contractors, but there should have been no need. To make matters worse, he had changed the password on the accounting software. I fixed the issue, and everybody got paid.

I was angry. I finished the day at work, stopped by a florist on the way home, and bought Molly a dozen roses. Things may not have been great at home, but at least it was home.

I did not even have the door open to the house before Molly was yelling. I pushed the door open, walked into the kitchen, slammed the roses onto the counter, and said, "I will never buy you flowers again. You've ruined the whole thing for me. I hate flowers now!"

I turned tail, walked out of the door—slamming it behind me—and burned rubber pulling out of the driveway.

Life sucked. What was the point?! I didn't head toward the crank dealer. He lived too far away, and it was not a sure thing.

I went straight to the crack cocaine dealer. I got high. Of course, I felt guilty later. I swore I would never do it again, but I got angry about something else a few weeks later. As an active addict, I always had my excuses—and any excuse would do.

I barreled down the road into a full-fledged drug-fueled addiction.

For those unfamiliar with the plague of addiction, it's not described well in your favorite TV show or movie. The media often shows the total depraved end to which addiction eventually leads: the loss of control, the complete disconnect with society, and the failure of all morals—the end or near it.

It is easy to sit on the other side of addiction and say, "I'll never do those things," or "That'll never be me." It's easy because the journey into the abyss doesn't happen overnight. A person does not start off stealing to support a habit, prostituting themselves, or sacrificing groceries for drugs. Although everyone ends up crossing lines, they thought they never would.

It would have been nice if I had come to grips with who I would become, the things I would do, and the regrets I would have to live with; however, like every single addict I have ever met, addiction, with its insidious nature, begins with a lie. But, it is not a lie to a parent, wife, child, sibling, relative, or friend.

We lie to ourselves. "I can handle this," stated with the bravado of an eight-year-old boy mounting a 2000-pound bull. That is an apt metaphor, for the bull wouldn't notice the 50 lbs. on his back for the first few moments and would stroll around. Still, once the bull figures out he has a passenger, no eight-year-old soul in this world could stay on for long, and when the bull goes into action, it will surely destroy the rider.

The spectator of the above illustration might do everything possible. The addict has no clue what's in store for him. "I can handle it." And they handle the drug use for a while. For some, it may be weeks, months, or years, but eventually, depending on the person and the substance or activity, that bull will start jumping, and what was a ride around the arena becomes a life-shattering, bucking, twirling, and twisting ride, only ending with the rider trampled underfoot.

Indeed, I would come heart-to-heart with my Creator, and He would give me life-altering faith, but in 2001, I was not there yet. So, instead, I rode around the proverbial arena, waving my hat at the crowd. This golden boy would fall within a couple of years, and life-shattering would be all I experienced.

Now, don't get me wrong. Although ups and downs would appear for spectators, it would not be up for 15 years.

Some would say recovery begins when we admit we cannot "handle it." Not so. I knew for a long time that handling the addiction was impossible. I accepted the failure. I was not willing to turn it over to God. I don't know if I knew how. Until the day I was arrested, I would have sworn I would die with cocaine in my system. What I had accepted was I was an addict with no hope.

I was near my end, but we are not at the end yet. I spent years trying to find a way to live while balancing my drug use with a regular life, and I succeeded for long periods.

An addict can find many ways to acquire money to support a drug habit. Stealing, borrowing, selling drugs, manufacturing drugs, pawning something, prostitution, panhandling, conning, and selling food stamps work. Except for prostitution, making and selling drugs, I have done all of those and then some.

I wouldn't say I liked most alternatives. The truth is most of the money-raising activities above resulted in jail time. I was not too fond of the thought of going back to jail. On the other hand, I am a fan of being able to open and close my door.

I am good at some of them.

I am smart enough to avoid the highest profit scheme above—manufacturing drugs. It doesn't take intelligence to manufacture substances. It takes a good recipe and organizational skills to follow it. You do not have to understand how chemicals work together. You don't have to know how a catalyst functions. You follow what others have done before you. Smart people leave the making of drugs to the idiots who think they are brilliant. For example, intelligence would steer anyone away from cooking certain kinds of methamphetamine. 1/1,000,000th part of one of the byproducts of red phosphorus crank in your air supply is fatal. I was not too fond of those odds. I have known several drug manufacturers in my life. I wouldn't trust most of them to manufacture a cup of boiling water without a recipe.

The penalty for being caught manufacturing drugs was steep, but the time awarded for selling drugs was as unacceptable. So, while the lure is strong because profits are high, stomaching the potential consequences was not something I wanted.

Prostitution? Well, that requires having something someone is willing to purchase–not a commodity I possess–unless I was ready to engage in homosexual activity, which I was not.

I was especially good at stealing. At times, I engaged in thievery. If authorities knew what I had gotten away with stealing, they would likely lock me up and throw away the key. The dollar figure is astounding, even staggering, but I participated in such activities for short periods. I didn't particularly appreciate stealing. It wasn't so much about guilt, as I enjoyed what I had accomplished earlier in life, and I wouldn't want anyone stealing from me.

I was left with work.

That also left me with several presumable impasses because some things were not worth losing, and others were worth having.

I had to find balance.

I would find some semblance of balance. When my wife could not and spent most of the last five years we were married in jail or rehab, I reserved time for dope after the kids were in bed. I helped with homework. I played with them. I performed in piano recitals with them. I cooked. My children achieved.

Miriam was at the top of her class when I was arrested and not allowed a bond. She went to state finals in tennis doubles in high school and won the Georgia Young Author's Award—recognized as the best writer in high school in Georgia two years in a row as a freshman and sophomore. In addition, she scored an almost unheard-of superior plus in National piano auditions. As her parent, I had taught her how to write, worked with her on piano and tennis, and helped with many science projects—including her state victory on blood-spatter analysis.

Paul seemed to suffer the most with the absence of his mother. He struggled in middle school until I found a Christian counselor for him. I worked with him. He pulled out of his slump and began to excel in school. He resumed his position as a straight-A student. He found a firm footing for his personality and started winning the hearts of those around him. He is the proverbial super-brilliant salesman.

Then there's my sweetheart-cuddle-bug Grace. She always seemed to maintain traction. If she has a flaw, it is that she never appreciated how beautiful and intelligent she is. The only school events I ever missed were not because of my addiction. At one point, I even sat on the parental advisory committee for her school. She has always done well. While I broke all three of their hearts, Grace has plugged on undaunted by the adversity that has plagued her life because of my mistakes.

I had great support from my parents. After a while, I moved into my parents' home. Dad needed help with my ailing mother, who had developed Alzheimer's. I needed help with my children. It was a good arrangement. Giving my three rides to piano lessons, practice for school performances, and church events gave Dad an opportunity away from the repressive responsibility of watching after Mom. When Dad needed assistance, I was present—whether he was ill with pneumonia or scheduling vacations and mission trips. My presence gave Dad some freedom.

When I eventually got a job requiring extensive travel, the kids had someone with whom to stay. Even on the road, however, I still helped with homework and had parent/teacher conferences on Skype and over the phone. In addition, I made it home for yet more duets at piano recitals and school events.

Support for being a single Dad stopped at home. People love to talk about "deadbeat Dads" or absent parents. I was anything but, yet I was plagued by assaults on my little family.

By this point, I had found some balance. The accusations against me did not concern my addiction. I hid it well from most people. No, others accused me of everything you can imagine. At one point, I was asked to step down from a volunteer position playing piano at a mission church—not because there was evidence, but because someone started a rumor I molested one of my daughters. It was a hatchet job by someone who did not like the music. I stepped down at the pastor's request, even though he knew my family well and would leave his children in my care. He knew the accusation had no substance. Keeping the peace was more important than the truth.

"You have no right to be raising two girls!"

"And why exactly?"

"Because you're a man."

So went part of the conversation between me and a social worker. Finally, not so politely, I escorted her out of my house, determined never to let them in my door again.

I was an overall good parent. The evidence was in the product—my children. That is how I felt, and to a large extent, it was true. What was also true was bits and pieces of me were dying daily.

Of course, while none of the accusations leveled at me were true, the truth, as I have said, was deeper-seated and had a grip internally that I thought I would never escape. I knew death would take me one day, and

I had no assurance other than it would be with cocaine in my system. I had no other hope of any different reality.

I worked. I parented. I got high.

April 11—8:00 am

I have done my best and made every attempt on all counts.

When I arrived at Lydia's house, there were two sheriff's deputies, and Lydia was waiting in the yard. I didn't bother approaching Lydia. I headed straight for the first deputy. He wanted to flex his authority, but I was utterly unthreatening in my tone of voice and posture. Momma didn't raise a fool. The first words out of my mouth were that I was leaving town because of the attempts on my life. I informed them I had been working for the DEA and Spelding County. I was afraid.

I was in enemy territory, but it was not the enemy who had a contract on my life. So, despite my concerns about Sheriff Marr, I hoped I could at least trust him to do the right thing.

I would not be able to speak with my two youngest. No one could say I did not try or had not attempted to notify law enforcement either. Still, I was sadly mistaken if I thought I would get any semblance of help here. I was a fool for trusting that help would come from anyone in law enforcement in this state.

As I write this, I am almost out of gas again in a church parking lot. This church would provide me with no assistance. I need to hit the road. I can make it another 20 miles. But I need to at least get out of this county. There's no telling what could happen to me here.

I am alone.

7

Mixed

Molly had been in and out of jail and rehab for five years. Upon her last release, I did not allow her back into the home. It was not an issue that she used. I used. I did not stand in judgment over her for her addiction. I stood as a barrier between her inability to control anything about her addiction and our children.

It had been years since our children received all their Christmas or birthday presents. Unable to control herself, she returned gifts to stores, and the money disappeared. She couldn't wait until nighttime to use. It was all or nothing. Not only did her use endanger and impact the kids, but it also threatened my ability to get high. In my mind, neither was fair game.

Molly had been released from jail and had moved into a house with two other women. My goal was to return her home if possible. I loved her, and the kids needed her. However, she could return home only by showing some restraint. This may sound like screwed-up thinking, but I was a using addict who had found a way to keep the dope in my life and still have what appeared to be an everyday life.

May 10 rolled around. My wife had not been out of jail for two months, had already missed probation appointments, and skipped a court date, so she had warrants again. We had been up most of the night using, and she couldn't go home because of the threat of arrest, so she rode to work with me, planning to sleep in my truck while I worked.

Two hours into my shift, my phone rang. It was my probation officer. I was on misdemeanor probation for a traffic violation. I was on probation with the same company Molly was. The officer gave me two hours to show up for a drug screen.

One of the drug addicts Molly lived with had reported us. I should never have been able to pass a drug screen. The dipstick must not have worked. As I was about to leave the office, my probation officer asked,

"Do you want to tell me where your wife is?"

I responded, "You know she doesn't live at home. I don't know where she is."

Two things were going through my mind. First, I had to be the luckiest guy on earth, and I wasn't about to do their job.

My officer turned to the police officer and said, "I have enough without this. Lock him up."

So much for the luck thing, but I loved Molly and wouldn't tell them anything. On our way back into town from my job, Molly proclaimed her love for me, "I don't care what anybody ever says or does; I will always choose you." With that in mind, I dropped her off at the library. "I don't know what's going to happen. If I don't come back, you know what happened."

I went to jail for refusing to tell on my wife. When my probation hearing rolled around, my dirty urine screen had returned from the lab, and the judge revoked the four months left on probation.

In a successful attempt to avoid going back to jail, Molly disappeared into yet another rehab. Two weeks after her "undying" proclamation of love, she was sleeping with one of the counselors in the rehab program. The kids stayed with Mom and Dad. My marriage came to a pragmatically practical end seventeen days after that proclamation and seventeen years after it began.

I exited jail with a broken heart. I had twenty dollars to my name. I walked away from lock-up, made a bee-line to my drug dealer, bought some crack, got high, and went home. When the kids came home from school, I had come down and was sane again. My broken life continued.

I got custody of the kids, and Molly continued disenfranchising them and then married the counselor.

Having gone through the sorrow of being a noncustodial parent with my first two children, I did everything possible to keep my youngest children's mother in their lives. I drove them to Atlanta to see their mom when she had no car. When they got a car, and the excuse was their vehicle broke down, I drove the kids to Atlanta and fixed her car on my dime. I forgave her for the debt when she failed to pay thousands in child support.

My actions towards my ex and her husband made their actions towards me so egregious, but it is not yet time to tell that part of my story.

I returned to my job as a maintenance and repairman for a McDonald's franchise. I earned the new owner's respect. I was promoted to head of maintenance for the entire franchise. I gained respect by saving them thousands in repair fees but not respect enough for decent pay. With sixty miles between the northernmost restaurant and the southern and having to drive at my own expense, I only kept the position for six months.

I went back into remodeling work for several rental property owners. The pay could have been better doing this, but it was all local, and I made it home every afternoon and evening to be with the kids and Mom.

It was a far cry from my "glory days" in the roofing industry, but in my stinted viewpoint, I had it all. I was a decent parent. I was able to be a good son and still use drugs, and even though I greatly limited my use, I did keep it in my life. That was paramount.

I was an excellent sibling. With my construction skills, I was able to help rescue one of my brothers from bankruptcy because 0f some ill-formed rental purchase decisions. I assisted my other brother in a rental disaster. I helped Dad take care of my sister's local property by keeping the lawn maintained and the gutters cleaned out.

No matter how hard I tried, the acceptance I had sought from my earliest childhood would not come. Instead, I would forever be the black sheep—outcast, unclean, unacceptable—I may as well have been a leper for all the ways family members looked at me, and it was not in my imagination. Verbal recriminations often accompanied the looks.

My family loved me. Make no mistake about it, but they had no clue how to breach the walls of isolation I had built around me. They share some blame because addiction has a Genetic component, and I come from a family of addicts who have never used drugs.

However, I am the one who does and should shoulder most of the blame if fault is what the world wants to assign. Addiction is an insidiously deceptive evil that crept into my life in increments. My addiction began early. I didn't express the addiction as a drug user until I was 25, but as I look back, what started as a small dysfunctional brokenness in childhood mushroomed into life-captivating enslavement, motivating all my decisions. Even what appeared to be good decisions in my own business were tainted by evil deception.

By not falling into my God-given purpose and following my Creator with all of my heart, I could not do the good I wanted. I always ended up doing the evil I did not want to do. However, an intelligent individual's sheer force of will kept this abhorrent isolationist's life afloat.

I might be intelligent and creative, but my ability to patch holes and bail water would end. I had, arguably, massive God-given talent, and it would take God moving in mighty ways to sink my ship but still save my life. Speaking of water, as God used a storm to turn around that helicopter to save Eve's life, God would use two well-timed storms to turn my life around—one would last but an hour or two, and the other would take up the better part of two days.

My phone rang. It was my best friend's son, Vick. His voice effusive with pleasure, he told me, "Uncle David. Do you know how you've helped me get jobs and hired me? I want to return the favor. I found us both a job if you're looking."

Within a few days, we were both hired. The only complication was I would be on the road quite often. But, after discussing it with my Dad and Miriam, it was a no-brainer. Miriam was now a sophomore and had helped with her younger siblings. She would man the fort on the home front, Dad was there to assist, and I had an opportunity to make some decent money.

In hindsight, it was not fair to place that kind of responsibility on Miriam's shoulders, but financially speaking, something had to give if we were to move back out of Dad's home. She was a super older sister and had proven her dedication and maturity over and over. But, of course, I should have remembered the damage others had done, and my absence would only weaken the fabric holding our tight-knit, at the time, little family together.

Once again, I could tell myself I had it all. It wasn't ideal, but I parented from a distance. We Skyped every night, and I assisted with homework through the online video service. I even attempted a parent/teacher conference over it. I sent Miriam grocery money every week. We were making it work.

Plus—it was a big plus; I found a way to use Google to find a drug dealer in every city I worked. As usual, I excelled at work and got high at night. I practiced the same rules on the road I did at home.

It was all cool with my young friend because we were the lone drug users in our families. His job lasted for two months when his drug use got the better of him. Admittedly, crack cocaine is hard to manage, but I already had figured it out. Vick was a multi-drug beaker on a Bunsen burner turned on high. I covered as long as possible, but it got the better of him.

I worked all over the eastern seaboard, going as far west as Texas and Oklahoma. It was awesome. I used my off time in the evenings to visit historical sites and museums. It was as if I were on a fabulous working vacation. And, without a problem, I found a dealer in every city, got high late every night, slept, and repeated it all the next day.

A memorable trip came in late summer. It was to be my longest time away from home. The schedule was three-and-a-half months long. It would take me from Virginia to Maine, west to New York, and back south again, hitting multiple hotels in every state between. It was an area of the country; being the history lover I am, I had always wanted to visit but had never had the opportunity. I was to be paid to tour the birthplace of freedom from Washington, D.C., to Boston, MA.

Late August brought me to Braintree, Massachusetts. I was wrapping up for the day when I looked up to see a not-quite-coherent young lady. She was homeless and coming down from a heroin trip. She needed somewhere to go. I had two beds in my hotel room. I gave her one for the night and told her we'd talk in the morning. Danielle crashed and burned. I forwent my usual high, stayed in, and got some rest myself. The following day, she told me she wanted to get clean. That was awesome to me—if she would do it, knowing, full well, I never could. I took the morning off and drove her three hours through Boston rush-hour traffic, dropped her at a rehab center, and promptly forgot all about her. She would not forget me.

I wrapped up the tour, came home in time for Thanksgiving, and took off again for a quick two-week stretch in Missouri, Oklahoma, and Texas. I was supposed to have a lovely leisurely few weeks off before hitting the road again after the new year began—this time for California. I never made it.

Miriam had gotten a job at a locally owned community favorite pizza parlor. It was a couple of days after Christmas. I drove her to work. Unfortunately, it started raining before she called me to pick her up, and this was no drizzle.

As I pulled into a parking spot by the door, I saw her sitting at a table reading. She didn't answer her phone. I honked the horn. She didn't look up. After waiting several minutes, staring at her oblivious figure through the window, I leaped out of the car. I was only about ten feet from the door. I was soaked to the skin before I got in.

I got about halfway to her reading refuge when, before I even realized it, I was staring at the ceiling. It resembled something from a cartoon. It wasn't funny, though. I had landed on my coccyx or tailbone. I broke it. California was going to have to wait. I could barely walk, much less service air-conditioners.

It wasn't all bad. I now had another excuse to buy some drugs.

Flash-forward a month. It was a Tuesday night. Mom and Dad were out of town. Tuesday night was the night for piano lessons. My children took lessons from Sid Skelton, my and my siblings' piano teacher, when we were children.

Many of my instructors were blessings in life, and Mr. Skelton was the apex example. A well-thought-of private piano instructor, this man traveled the country judging the instruction of other teachers. As a result, he has been noted as one of the best in the country.

Mr. Skelton was hard-core. It was not unusual for him to pop my hands with a ruler or pull the tiny hairs on the back of my head. He often used these disciplinary tactics to drive home a specific point about keeping our fingers curled or remembering certain passages. Not so oddly, my sister remembers not many occasions such as I experienced, but then again, she practiced. The temporary pain he inflicted was not nearly as painful to me as practicing. Otherwise, I would have practiced more. I've often wished he had inflicted a tad more as I struggled with piano playing later in life.

By the time my children began taking from him, Mr. Skelton had mellowed with the change in societal norms about how private instructors should treat children. Gone were the ruler taps and hair pulls.

Instead, he had found effective but kinder and gentler ways, or was it when I quit he didn't need those harsh measures anymore? There may be days that try men's souls, but I was the child that tried his.

Back to the present tense of my story: I dropped my two youngest at piano lessons. Within ½ a block of Mr. Skelton's house was "Cocaine Corridor." An officer told me more cocaine was sold on a nearby street in Griffin, Georgia, than in all other locations in the county combined.

It was too convenient for me. It would not be prudent to pick up my nightly supply while I had the kids with me, so while I did not have them, I drove around the block, bought my $20 worth, and headed home. I would not make it.

I was within ½ mile from home when the blue lights flashed behind me. I was far from a drug neighborhood by then. I absentmindedly dropped my dope in the ashtray and shut it—something I had never done. It's always easier to eat the drugs than get arrested for possession. When I realized my foolishness, it was too late—an officer was at my window telling me to step out of the car.

A series of questions ensued. "Why were you in that neighborhood?" I had that one covered. "What did you do with the crack you just bought?" I did not have to answer. "May we search your vehicle?" And I had a clear answer, "No." I knew the law. I was not on probation. They had no legitimate probable cause. They could not search my vehicle without my permission, and they had not stopped me with a K-9 unit, so I was home-clear. I was, legally, untouchable. Of course, since when did that matter to the police?

"Call for a K-9 unit," the lieutenant hollered at an officer.

I quickly pointed out the fallacy of the command, "You do know that is illegal. You cannot detain me on the side of the road and call for a K-9 unit. You can't use a K-9 unless you pull me over with one."

Smug-smile-lieutenant responded, "There has been some recent case law about it; I know what you're saying, but I don't really care. We're going to do this, and you can complain about it later."

Then he turned around again and yelled, "Tell the K-9 unit to bring a ticket book because none of us have one," as if he thought it would justify an illegal detainment, or perhaps he thought it fooled me.

The K-9 unit showed up, and the dog did not alert anywhere on my vehicle, but they proceeded to search my van anyway. It took them about 15 minutes of searching, but they found my drugs.

I was going to jail, and the ride was about as painful as you can imagine. The tailbone was healing, but the seat was a steel seat in a cramped steel cage in the K-9 unit SUV. I felt like a dog, but all hope was not gone. I will be out in a couple of days.

Well, no, I wouldn't. I was denied bond. You would have thought I was some big, bad criminal. Plenty of career criminals continuously get bonds, but not me. While the legal community may have thought they had reasons, they were as illegal as my arrest had been, and I got no help from my court-appointed attorney.

Whatever man often thinks, God usually has something else in His purpose. The bottom line was I had experienced my last cocaine high. God could not deal with my deeper issues if I were juiced on the drug. It began a resurgence of God's dominion over my life. I was a purchased child of His, and He had plans for me to prosper within His will and not to fail. God needed to straighten out an errant child—me—and it would be a process—one beginning with a storm, soaking me to the skin and providing a slippery restaurant floor, in turn, breaking my tailbone, leaving me in town to be illegally arrested and detained by a judge. That process would be realized in yet another torrential downpour as I left my hometown—destination unknown.

Once again, though, we are not there yet. The second storm would come over two years later—after losing everything I owned, and all hope in my abilities.

April 11—9:00 am

As I was wondering what I would do, my phone rang. It was Lydia. She claims to have had a change of heart and will let me see Paul and Grace.

I doubt it!

She has offered to meet me at a local grocery store. I realize I am walking into a trap. Lydia is a lot of things, but make this kind of turnaround in this short a time? Probably not in a million years, certainly not in less than an hour.

However, I am running out of options. If this is a trap involving law enforcement, I must show up—even though I am sure nothing good will come.

I must never allow Lydia the option of telling Paul and Grace that I did not show up. If I do not go, she will use it as an opportunity to tear down their spirits. No matter what else in life, my children will always know I show up if there is a chance I can see them—even to my detriment.

8

A Little Bit of That

In jail, I sat. My children and my new career were hanging in the balance—not that too many people were interested in what was happening to me. Some claimed to be concerned with my children, and a few were.

As I waited, for there is nothing else to do in jail, I contemplated my kids' situation. As a family, we had been through much—not including the obvious impact of drugs. The only other person who had been around through our trials was, for all practical intents and purposes, gone, but Molly had been there.

Ten years earlier, September 6, 2005, started grand and glorious. Molly and I were up at 4 a.m., and by 5, we headed to Terre Haute, 15 miles from where we lived in Clinton, Indiana, at the time. The cause for our early jaunt? We had a scheduled Caesarian Section scheduled.

One to make the most fun out of given situations, I sped through the deserted streets of Terre Haute. With no traffic and a very pregnant wife with me, I had an excuse if we got pulled over for speeding. We had the radio on loud, and we laughed and joked the whole way.

The C-section went off without a hitch. I left the newly named Grace in the care of a nurse. To close her up, Molly was knocked out, and I walked back to the room with my incapacitated wife on her bed.

No sooner had we arrived, but a nurse knocked on the door and pulled me out of the room to provide privacy from my mother-in-law, who had been waiting in recovery.

"Mr. Riordan, Dr. Contreras is with Grace. We have a problem. Grace stopped breathing. The doctor was able to resuscitate her, but she can not breathe on her own. Her lungs are not fully developed. She is in the NICU. She is alright for now. You cannot hold her. The slightest touch could be too much excitement and cause her to go into cardiac arrest."

I don't think I'd ever seen anything quite so pitiful as my little girl laying under the tent—little chest struggling to rise as she fought for her life, monitor wires crisscrossing her tiny frame and tubes running into her mouth and nose.

For a week, we had to observe Grace through hardened plastic. Then, finally, she pulled through, and our fears were alleviated. Mother and child came home, but it had been a rough week taking its toll on everyone.

A week later, I returned to a dark house from work on a Friday night. This was a little unusual, but I assumed Molly and the kids were visiting Molly's mother, who lived about a mile away. No biggie. I checked the phone for messages. There was one.

"Mr. and Mrs. Riordan, this is Dr. Contreras. Your son's test results came in today. I need you to call me back tonight." She then left her home phone number.

I don't know about you, but when a physician leaves her home phone number on your answering machine, it must be urgent, and this was about Paul—not Grace.

The phone did not touch the cradle between calls, and Dr. Contreras answered on the first ring. If I hadn't been worried yet, that would have gotten me. My nerves, already stretched from Grace's ordeal, were about to snap!

All I had known was Paul had been to see the doctor about some mosquito bites he had been scratching, and he had developed impetigo. Dr. Contreras filled in the details. Then, with only a stethoscope, the good doctor had heard a swooshing sound she didn't like and had ordered an ultrasound of his heart. I will never forget her words on the phone, "Mr. Riordan, your son needs more extensive tests. I am not calling this an emergency tonight, but this needs to happen in the next couple of weeks, or your son could die."

Not an emergency? I don't know whose dictionary she uses, but you tell me one of my children's lives is at risk, and I'll consider it an emergency. Thank you very much.

I called Molly's cell. No answer.

I called my mother-in-law. No answer. I called every number I had—no Molly.

I hopped in my truck and ran over to my mother-in-law's. The lights were off, but she answered. "No, I only know Molly called me earlier and told me she was in a safe place."

I am out of metaphors for where my nerves were at that point. No words describe it. I am glad I did not know my mother-in-law was lying. I may have done something I would have regretted.

Throw into the mix Grace's trying post-birth experience, postpartum depression from Molly, and now Paul's uncertain future. I should have lost all touch with reality. I didn't.

Molly's mom, who had long tried to break us up, had seized the opportunity while my wife struggled with postpartum depression to hatch a plan. She had secreted Molly in a home for battered women to gain false ammunition. I have powerful feelings about men who hurt women to the extent I once broke a man's arm for hurting a young lady on a dance floor. So, I am still upset about this attempt at a false accusation by my ex-mother-in-law.

The long and short of it is that two weeks of misery later, Molly and I met up at a cardiologist's office. My three-year-old son had a condition called coarctation of the aorta. The only remedy was to operate, cut out part of the aorta, stretch it, sew it back together, and pray no scar tissue formed, resulting in his death or a repeat of the surgery.

The surgeon's office informed us the surgeon did more coarctation surgeries than anyone else. Therefore, this surgery would be "routine" for him. I mistakenly asked, "How many surgeries of this kind has he done?" The surgeon's assistant responded, "He does 6-8 of these a year." I silently stared because I don't know where these doctors find their definitions, but you do routine every day, not once every two months.

For all the routine non-emergency status of my son's condition, the doctor insisted he needed to operate within a couple of days!

One interesting note: while my 3-year-old son lay in recovery, he looked up at me and said, "You didn't have to worry. Jesus told me to sit on His lap. He told me everything was going to be okay." My son was not prone to make things up back then. He wasn't a teenager yet. I believed my son believed it, which was okay with me. I do not doubt this happened to my son. God's actions toward me have altered how I see things. You may understand in a little while why I say this.

Throughout this ordeal, I had no real moral support from anyone except perhaps my mom and dad, who showed up when Molly disappeared, informing me at the time that it was my fault. However, they did stay until Paul was home from the hospital. They were supportive in their own way.

Back to my present, I could not depend on my parents this time.

Mom, whose passion had always been children, was beyond the ability to care—locked deep inside the throes of Alzheimer's. Dad cared deeply, but his attention, as it should have been, was devoted to the love of his life, who was swiftly deteriorating. My siblings? Well, they had issues vital to them.

No one had a chance to respond, for Miriam, the oldest of my youngest three, had made a choice steeped in lies told to her by her older sister, Lydia.

Lydia, my second child with my first wife, had been scheming for about two years. Her deep-seated hatred of me at the time went back to two things—one was beyond my control, and the other was entirely within my power, and I did not make the wrong decision. Still, Lydia developed a hatred of her father that morphed into a desire to destroy everything about me. I provided ample fodder.

The first goes back to the repercussions of a pre-marriage pregnancy. When my first marriage ended, the divorce did not go how my first wife's father thought it should have. Jeanette couldn't bring herself to admit to her father she had been unfaithful to me and had done so with at least one man and a woman. It was the second one causing consternation, and I had her lover admitting to the relationship on tape.

It didn't matter in the end because when she remarried, she did so to the sheriff's son of her hometown. They abused the law frequently, and as I have recounted, it took two years of their legal contempt for me to defeat them in court, but they damaged me and my girls. For two years, my ex told the kids I was not coming to pick them up, I wasn't paying child support, and I didn't love them. She twisted their impressionable minds to create enmity between my two oldest children and me. It distanced me from my oldest, a daddy's girl. It made a vengeful, dysfunctional schemer in my youngest—a mommy's girl.

The second situation occurred about the time Lydia was 19.

Grace and Paul healed and recovered; both were doing better than okay. Molly had gotten through the worst of the postpartum depression, and we were making some attempt to repair the damage her mother had done to our relationship.

Lydia called me out of the blue. She had emancipated herself at the not-so-mature age of 16. She was currently on a siesta from a methamphetamine binge and needed somewhere to stay. I told her she was welcome to stay with us, and I flew her to Indiana.

There was to be only one absolute rule. We could work around anything except when it concerned Lydia's safety and that of her smaller siblings. She needed to think through her decisions and ensure nothing she did would harm the kids.

Family members back in Georgia placed their bets. The most anybody gave Lydia was two days. To her credit, she lasted two weeks.

One afternoon, we came walking into the house. I had set Grace down on the floor in her car seat. In stormed Lydia; she was pitching a temper tantrum worthy of a five-year-old. She kicked a shoe across the room through the air, missing Grace's head by barely an inch. The shoe had not stopped moving before I had Lydia by the arm with one hand and her backpack in the other. I walked her out the door, turned around, reentered the house, and locked the door behind me.

If she had attempted to knock on the door, ask forgiveness, or anything else, I would have worked something out with her and given her another chance. She is my daughter, and I still love her. She didn't want that chance. She walked away, and the seeds of discontent planted by her mother flowered into a full-bloomed hatred of her father.

Confusion and chaos, the sins of the parents, and current choices rained destruction and sufficient blame for all involved.

Sitting in the jail, contemplating the mess I had made of things, I began searching for answers as to what to do with the children. Mom's health was diminishing, and Dad couldn't handle anything more. Amid these thoughts, I received a summons to juvenile court.

True to form, Lydia didn't visit the jail and work it out with me. No, she wanted her opportunity to shine and make me out to be as bad as possible. The bailiffs dragged me into the juvenile court building in full jail regalia, complete with handcuffs, shackles, and a black-and-white striped jumpsuit.

Lydia got guardianship of all three. She was the hero of the day. Miriam had called her the hour I got locked up, revealing the whole sisterhood bond and closeness thing. It would only take about two months for the both to betray each other and by Miriam's 17th birthday, six months away, Lydia would lose Miriam. In addition, she would be responsible for scarring her little sister for life.

Back at the jail, the D.A. offered a deal involving only probation. There would be no prison. I could probably beat the charges, but with no bond and the D.A.'s propensity to drag things out, I'd still be in jail for a year or two. My quickest way out from behind bars was a 9-month RSAT program or Residential Substance Abuse Treatment. I was to be sent to South Georgia and enrolled in the Turner RSAT program. I had to stay in jail until a bed opened, which would take about three months.

Georgia had taken a proactive approach to drug addiction. The state repurposed several former prisons and re-staffed them with addiction counselors and, of course, the obligatory guards. Make no mistake about it; it may not have been called a prison anymore, but you know what they say, "If it walks like a duck and quacks like a duck, then it must be a duck." What it wasn't by label, it was in reality.

I found the program material to be excellent. It was informative and helpful. The program's administration, though, left a great deal to be desired. They did succeed in one thing, as far as I was concerned. I would rather die than go back through the ordeal again. When I completed the program, I wasn't sure I didn't want to die.

Hell had been unleashed onto my life, hitting me one assault after another.

The first came early on. At some point during my first incarceration, I encountered tuberculosis. I tested positive and proceeded to take all the medication the doctor prescribed. This would make me immune to that deadly bloody lung disease, but I would always test positive for it.

When I tested positive for tuberculosis at Turner RSAT, they wanted to follow up with a chest x-ray.

The chest x-ray came back with spots on my lungs and, in turn, indicated the need for an MRI of my chest at Augusta Medical Prison. The test results revealed there was a good chance I had lung cancer. It would require another trip back to Augusta to see an oncologist.

Out of the blue, I got a request for a conversation with Lydia. Miriam had run away from home. She had packed up her stuff, left, and headed to her best friend's house in Marietta, Georgia—3 hours from Lydia. Lydia could do nothing about it. It would be several weeks before I found out why she ran away. Lydia left out the "minor" detail that her husband had sexually assaulted Miriam, and when she did tell me, she laid the blame at Miriam's feet. I'm not sure how a minor holds any responsibility when a forty-year-old is involved, but now I had a daughter scarred by sexual abuse and her two younger siblings bereft of the structure Miriam provided. As long as Miriam had been around, I worried less about the other two. Now, she was broken, and they were alone.

I have but one word to describe how I felt: helpless, and I was for the moment. When I successfully graduated from RSAT, perhaps I could do something—if I defeated cancer.

And the hits just kept on coming.

The only consistent rule of RSAT was to ensure you never stand on firm ground. If you were disruptive, you were acting out your addiction in addictive personality traits. If you followed the rules and did well with your lessons? Guess what? Yeah, you got it. You were acting out your addiction in addictive personality traits. The one thing you could count on was they would do their best to knock you off your feet daily, and God forbid if you were intelligent and well-behaved!

The RSAT administrators gave time extensions like candy at a children's convention, though I can promise you they were not received like said candy. When they could not inflame my passions and get me to break a rule, they concocted a rule violation to motivate my anger. I had seen it coming, and they would not win, but I had no way to win except to accept. I was lucky to graduate only one week late, and that was because of my second trip to the Augusta State Medical Prison. When they could not make me act out, they moved on to far easier targets and left me to the misery I had returned to after my second trip to Augusta, but it was not out of kindness and concern they left me alone for my last couple of months.

I was more than halfway home. Seven-and-a-half months had passed since my arrest. I was about to move from Phase Two to Phase Three in RSAT. I was halfway through the rehab program when I got the midnight tap from an officer. I headed back to Augusta.

Since my trip fell near a holiday weekend, no matter what, I would end up in Augusta for a couple of extra days. I knew it would add a week to my RSAT time, although I had some unrewarded hope the administrators would be more kind.

A regular prison is entirely different when you've been in an RSAT. Arriving in my assigned dorm, I discovered anything was available. Drugs flowed like the Biblical reference of milk and honey. I had no worries because drug tests are mandatory upon return to RSAT, and I was not that big of a fool.

After a couple of gut-wrenching days, my oncologist appointment arrived. Officers called me out of the dorm to stand in line with about 20 other cancer patients. The line was unimportant, however, because the doctor was using his list instead of the line to determine the order called. But, of course, someone must be last. That day, it was me.

"Mr. Riordan, I waited to call you last because I have little to say. Someone made an error reading your test results. You do not have lung cancer. You do have Non-alcoholic Fatty Liver Disease, but I am not qualified to speak with you about that. Since you will be out of RSAT in the next few months, I recommend waiting until you are on the outside to deal with it. It won't cause you any significant issues for a while yet." So much for months of worrying about cancer, but my relief was palpable. If I didn't have to worry about the other for a while yet, I sure wasn't about to worry about it now!

The oncologist appointment was on a Thursday. I doubted I would be shipped back to Turner County until Tuesday. Monday was Labor Day. Since almost everyone in the dorm was using drugs, it would be a long weekend. It would be longer than I expected.

I was hesitant to call anyone. I had not discussed my impending official cancer diagnosis with anyone. I tried calling my dad over the weekend but could not reach him or anyone else. Finally, I called Miriam on Sunday, September 4, in desperation to talk to someone. To my surprise, she was at her granddad's. However, she quickly handed the phone to my dad rather than speak to me.

"Son, your mother has just gone to Heaven to be with Jesus. I was holding her hand when she took her last breath. I have called the ambulance, and we're waiting for them to come and take her to the funeral home."

"Timing is everything," they say. I was not at RSAT. It would take a quick phone call from someone in my family to ensure I make it to the funeral. It would take a minor miracle to arrange it. With my dad's proclamation, the most intelligent, passionate, incredible woman I had ever known, and at this point in my life, my only fan, passed from my life. No one called to arrange for me to attend the funeral, and the miracle did not happen.

Dad did say later that if I had let him know, he would have moved mountains to get me to the funeral, and I know him; he would have. I would never have asked it of him. The love of his life had just managed to "shuffle off this mortal coil," His and my mother's relationship remains the most remarkable love story I've witnessed. I would suffer this loss alone, surrounded by men high and hiding from their pain. It was a fitting and just place for me.

April 11—10:00 a.m.

It was, indeed, a trap, and it was, of course, sprung by my daughter and made possible by yet another betrayal. Aaron made sure Dad never got my letter. Dad had reported the R.V. as stolen. However, there is no warrant sworn out for me.

I was surrounded by 5 or 6 sheriff cars when I pulled up to Lydia's promise of being able to say goodbye to Paul and Grace.

I explained my tenuous situation to the officers, and of course, they mocked me while they handcuffed me.

They all had a good laugh at me.

My only hope is in Officer Greg Clerke. He is the only one I still trust who works for Spelding County. He is seconded to the DEA and knows most of what I have gone through. Yet, at the very least, he has always appeared sympathetic to me.

Greg was my first phone call. He proceeded to make excuses. First, I should not have taken Dad's R.V. without express permission. He further explained that the first thing I should have done, legally, after taking the R.V. was to report my situation to an officer of the law. Mmm. Isn't that what I did?

9

Kneaded

I finished RSAT. I spent 368 days behind bars and determined it would be my last.

I had participated heavily in the independently led church in the RSAT program, and I wanted to have a good relationship with my God and Creator. I had committed my heart to Him at an early age, but I had spent a large portion of my life with cocaine coursing through my veins.

"Do not be filled with wine in excess, but be filled with the Spirit," so wrote Paul the apostle. That applied to my substance of choice, cocaine. It would be easy to get "coke." I only had to make the call. I didn't. While I genuinely did not see an easy way out, I committed never to call my crack dealer again. There is a colloquial expression in A.A., "white-knuckling," which would become my way of life. The term comes from holding on so tight your knuckles turn white. If I were to stay clean, I resolved to make it my daily practice if that's what it took. It would be a miserable way of life, but I was not going back to jail, nor would I fail my children again.

Dad made me an offer on my way home from RSAT. It was Generous, considering everything I had put him through. I would live at the house, and he would pay me a small stipend, and I would remodel his home. My skills are substantial. He would receive a quality product. It was Generous because, while he had faith in my construction abilities, my life failures had left him with many doubts about what direction my life would go.

He would be satisfied with my construction achievements on his house. I still had plenty to learn about life. I was still in the mindset that remaking myself was a possibility. On this end, God would give me enough rope to hang myself.

I hit the ground running. Work was progressing well on the house. The two most challenging parts of any construction project are starting and finishing. But, I quickly overcame the issues of getting started. Of course, many problems arose along the way, and it was a considerably large project. There was no surface in the house I would not touch—some required tearing out and replacing—but I had the necessary skill and was in my element.

Early in the project, Dad had a mission trip planned. He was headed to Equatorial Brazil to help build a church. While I learned the basics of painting from my father, painting was the only construction skill he had to teach. Dad participated in many mission trips. He more than made up for what he lacked in skill with the heart and soul he put into it.

At any rate, he would be gone for two weeks. (That deep rumble you hear in the background rising to a crescendo is the auditory hint that something terrible is about to happen).

I determined I would tackle the single most significant part of the job while he was gone—the kitchen floor. It was good timing for such a project because I would have to turn the whole house upside down to do the job, and Dad would be gone.

I planned and prepared. I would replace some floor joists, subfloor, underlayment, and finished floor. My goal, as always, was to do an outstanding job, including spending the least money on top-shelf products. It would be my Dad's last hurrah to fix up his home. I was dedicated to doing my best and skilled at finding great material deals.

I did not let him down. We spent the week before he was to leave shopping for, transporting, and unloading lumber, nails, thin set, and grout for the floor. We also got paint and fixtures, switch and outlet plates, and outlets and switches. Then, it was "Game On!" so to speak. I was ready.

Dad caught his plane. I surveyed the kitchen, moved everything out of the kitchen, grabbed my demolition tools, and my phone rang.

It was Vick. (Bum-bum-buuuuuum). (Impending-doom-musical-crescendo hits its peak and falls to eerie silence).

My young friend, God loves him, and so do I; he requires an introduction!

There are two things you should know about Vick. The first is that he and I had had a working relationship for about seventeen years, above and beyond just being his adopted uncle. I hired him to work for me when I was a contractor and then as an employee at a couple of companies I managed. For the most part, I had always been happy with his performance for a while with each opportunity. He returned the favor by helping me get the job with the PTAC company a few years earlier.

The second, you already know. Vick was the only other "family" member who chose substances as an outlet for addiction.

It all started for Vick much earlier in life than it did for me—while he was in middle school, for it had become popular at his middle school to take Ritalin.

In true addict fashion, his use grew with time. It became preferable to be high than to live normally. By the time he was 16, staying up high all weekend was the "in" thing within his circle of friends.

Now, this is no honest reflection on his parents. My best friend had become a rather acclaimed church musician. He and his wife, Laurie, successfully raised five other incredible children. Addiction is devious and sneaks into the best of families regardless of parenting skills. Since most do not notice illicit drug use early, it grows without restriction for some time.

The first bump in the road for Vick came at 16; only it was more than a bump. He had been awake since Friday morning. Sunday after church, Dan and Laurie had other things to do, and they gave the van keys to Vick because he admitted to being tired. So, he would go home ahead of the rest of the family.

Within a few miles, young Vick was asleep at the wheel and crossed over the center line, hitting another car head-on. No one died, but people were injured in the other vehicle while Vick walked away with bruises. He made excuses and got away with it. Dan paid increased insurance premiums for years.

Within another year or so, Vick had graduated to methamphetamine and had learned how to support his habit by "slinging" dope, and he was pretty good at it.

Becoming a dealer and user of methamphetamine would dominate his life for the next 17 years. He wouldn't stop with the meth, either. Like me, he never felt comfortable in his own skin, and soon, any substance would do, so long as he was high.

Over those 17 years, he was arrested many times and shared another distinction within our family with me. He became a convict. He became one on multiple occasions.

We shared addiction. We shared conviction. We had an affinity for each other, and Vick was my best friend's son, for after my mother's passing and my subsequent release from RSAT, Dan and I became much closer. As adult brothers, we had grown close. After my discharge, we bonded even tighter, and he became the one person I could always count on. He was not only my brother; he became my best friend.

As I have said, Vick and I have much in common. We both chose to act out our addictive personality disorders by using drugs. Some people choose food and become excessively overweight. Some choose to exercise and run vast numbers of miles every week in their pursuits to make inner demons flee, to the extent they damage their bodies—sometimes permanently. Some people work 60-100 hours every week to the detriment of their families. Some people do all the above; even if you exclude drugs, you still have a dysfunctional addict. Substances put a much dirtier spin on things, but to the wife and child at home alone without husband and father, the cause matters less than the absence.

An addict is an addict—it doesn't matter, in the greater scheme of things, how we act it out. Addiction is our way of avoiding a relationship with our Creator and others. Some people justify their addictions by societal standards. However, for the individual, it is still about not having a relationship or only having a limited relationship with God. So, addicts plod through life, going from one dysfunction to another if they never address their issues with their Creator. Everything they do is tainted and stained. They view everything through the tinted glass of self-absorption, the craving, the need to put on a salve, and the inner demand to fill a hole.

As a Christian, I had thrown dirt in the hole. That is what protected me through the years. God had me. He had my back—even in the depths of my drug use.

As evidence of God's active presence in my life, I can recall a moment when I first started using. I was at a friend's house, and we were definitively high. I had just hit my crack pipe and was experiencing the initial euphoric rush when my friend said something about Jesus.

A crack high doesn't last long, but the effects can linger for about an hour. At the mention of Jesus, I was immediately "stone cold" sober, for a second had not elapsed. It was immediate. I spoke, and while voluntary, the words were not mine. For thirty to forty-five minutes, we discussed the difference Christ would make in his life. For those minutes, neither of us touched the dope or the pipe.

This God Appointment illustrates that nothing would have stopped this man from getting the message—whether he chose to act on it or not was his decision; however, he would hear the words if he sat in that room with me. So, with the message stated, we resumed getting high. I never saw him again, and I don't remember his name. He lived in the same apartment building with me and mysteriously moved the day after our shared God Appointment.

I can also remember several times when God's divine protection was evident. This kind of thing did not happen once or twice either—as I said, "several" times—and every time where my potential destruction was imminent except twice. One example I recall was during one of my stints in jail. I was trying. I led a daily Bible study. I don't remember what precipitated the anger flair-up from another inmate, but the long and short of it was I was dangling at the end of the arm of a nasty dude who was about to rearrange my face.

With his arm drawn back and fist tightened, the guy froze with a look of complete confusion. He dropped the front of my jumpsuit. He dropped his raised fist, turned around, and walked away. The guy was not a man who walked away from a fight—notably a sure win, which I am sure he thought he had.

Later the same day, he was suddenly removed from the cell block and released from jail because of an error made by a deputy in his paperwork.

Protected, yeah, I had divine protection from others so many times that the look on their faces was indistinguishable from each other, and I recognized it for what it was. One of the times I was not protected occurred a year after my drug rehabilitation release and related to what was ahead.

I have been heavenly protected many times from catastrophic events. One time, years ago, before I began curbing my drug use, my wife and I had been awake for two weeks straight before we ran out of dope. When you are coming down from crack, nothing else matters except getting more. She said she could not drive, so I hopped in the car with, to my utter regret, two of my children. I made the twenty-mile drive to pick up some more dope.

I was fine until I was on my way back. I was traveling southbound on 19/41, going about 60 mph, when my body did what a body should do after two weeks of no sleep. It shut down. I awakened as my car crossed the ditch in the median. I was now going south on the northbound side of a major highway, with cars passing me on both sides going north. The closing speed was about 120 mph. Miraculously, I got the car back into the median, blowing all four tires. No one was injured, yet I had come close to killing myself, my children, and people in at least 15 or twenty cars.

Consequently, this made me want to control my drug use, and I never went on a binge like that again. I got my dope and my children out of the car—walking away—narrowly missing the police, who showed up minutes later! Divine protection was the order of the day. Not so in November 2017, but that comes later.

Anyway, enter my young friend, my best friend's son.

Into this historical and familial environment, my cell phone ringing shattered the air.

Vick called me. He figured, and rightfully so, that I'd talk to him. Most of the members of my family had given up on him. I was the last man standing because we shared a common affliction. I did not look down my nose at him. He needed to borrow a vehicle. He said he did not have transportation and was trying to get a job. Truth be told? I knew better, but I also wanted him to know I cared.

My car made it back when he said. It was to be the only time that ever happened. Thus began a short period of vehicle loaning. Invariably, the times he needed my car got later and later during the day until it became a nighttime adventure. All subterfuge disappeared. He offered to pay me in methamphetamine to "rent" my car. I accepted. Yes, I was on probation, and a dirty urine screen would destroy it, but enjoying a bit of high was okay in my book. It wasn't crack cocaine, and I was not fond of the high enough to use it all the time. Meth made me feel toxic. I gave some away, and the fact is he rarely paid. I mistakenly thought keeping an open line between us was better for him.

Payment stopped after a couple of times because he found I would loan him the car without charge. I sincerely wanted to find a way to help him. I was in no great danger of using coke anymore—and the meth wasn't around to use most of the time, and when it was, I didn't like the after-effects and wondered why I had used any at all.

A few weeks went by. I had begun work on the house, and soon, Dad was leaving the country for a mission trip. He would be gone for a couple of weeks. I thought, "I can help." I agreed to let him and his current female sidekick stay at the house. The cunningness of addiction is baffling. Rather than help, I did nothing that came close and instead got drawn in. He paid. To my shame now, I used and, as usual, despised the after-effects.

A couple of months went by. I didn't pursue the meth. It wasn't my thing, and I knew better than to use coke. I had decided it was a dead-end course. I maintained. Vick got transportation. Vick lost said transportation. Dad had to go on another mission trip. I wanted to help again. This time, there would be no dealing around me. I was going to put my foot down. I failed.

Then, something I had no experience with happened. My young friend and his girlfriend used GHB. Vick lost his mind. One night, in a fit of un-precipitated rage, he attacked me. I assumed the meth had finally broken his mind. It did not end well for him. I may be older, but it was a construction worker amid over-full-time employment against a g'd-out, doped-out meth head who hadn't hit a lick in years. I did not hurt him, but I kept him from harming me. He is my best friend's son. Damaging him would never be my motivation—even after this night. After I let him up, he ran into the kitchen and threatened me with a large kitchen knife. I dodged his feeble attempts and walked outside after telling him to leave.

"Just give him space," is what I told myself. Then, as I pittled around in my car, I heard someone walk up behind me. When I turned around, Vick had a loaded 44 pointed at my face. "From this distance, you really can't miss—and you better not because before your hand recovers from the kickback, I'll have it, and that gun shoved up your …." His finger trembling on the trigger, the familiar confused look pouring over his face; Vick lowered the weapon and walked up the street.

I was done. I had some value for my brain left. Drugs were not something with which to be trifled. I had, on the surface, known better. This occasion gave me a concrete, real-world example of why. I would have it in three more days if I needed another reason.

Dad came home on Saturday. On Sunday morning, he got a call from a credit card company—the credit card company handling Dad's credit card I carried. "Son? Handle this." I listened. A ton of charges that were not mine were in the statement. As the customer service rep went down the list, a particular hotel had multiple listings. It was Vick's favorite hotel at the moment. It was the card I carried. Vick or his latest partner had somehow stolen the number. There was no way I would come out of this unscathed. I didn't know what to do. Since all the purchases were in Griffin, and a charge was made that morning, Dad called the police. I waited. It wasn't long before my phone began going off.

"Uncle David! Please tell this policeman you permitted me to use the card. I'll pay you. I promise. Just give me 24 hours." "Vick. I can't and won't, but let me see what I can do." On went my creative thinking hat. I had already reported the charges as fraudulent. The policeman was overworked and susceptible to a smooth talker. I talked the policeman into not pursuing anything for 24 hours, explaining that I would handle it with the credit card company if they returned the money.

So many things whirled in my head. The downside of Vick being arrested for stealing Dad's credit card information was huge—major and cataclysmic. There was no upside. This situation would be a significant balancing act. Lying to people is easy. Scamming and making it long-term is very difficult. It is the biggest reason I would not try to pull a long con on my worst days. When it unravels, you have a veritable mess!

Anybody can lie. A few can get away with it. I had a 15-year history of pulling off a long con—failing at the beginning and a massive success for a while but unraveling at the end. So, I knew what it meant to try. Most long cons last because people are either too stupid or ignorant, too lazy, or too busy to discover it, which is usually something they don't want to know anyway.

At this point, there was a fine line of separation between the policeman, my Dad, and the credit card company. I had to manage the situation. A fine line separated me from problems—problems from which I could extricate myself. Vick never would, and the consequences within the family would be enormous. Dad and the policeman were at once both too busy and slightly ignorant. The credit card company was too lazy. Vick would never pay, but things didn't have to explode with the suitable slight manipulation. I managed the situation.

Now, at least Vick was gone. I did not have to worry about him anymore. I had nothing I could do to help him; on a personal level, it was too dangerous for me. Inevitably, I would end up back with coke.

There was no chance any sane individual would restore lines of communication after pointing a loaded gun in my face and stealing the credit card information. I wasn't worried.

April 11—11:00 a.m.

Greg has told me he'll handle it as best he can. I just needed to be patient.

Patient? Yeah, right! I am sitting in a jail holding cell managed by a sheriff who has despised both me and the law in the past, at least as far as I am concerned. His reputation is not lily-white in his community.

However, patience is the most prudent thing I can have.

Rest is what I need. I am exhausted. Currently, there's no warrant. Greg has intimated there will not be one forthcoming. Hate me or not, Sheriff Mick Marr can only legally hold me for 72 hours without a warrant. I, at the very least, can get some much-needed rest.

I informed the jailer I needed my heart and diabetes medicines. It'll be interesting to see how long it takes to see a doctor.

10

Proofed

Success in life is what everybody wants. How we define success is what differs from person to person. How to attain success is also varied, but, as I have told my children, I have narrowed it down to an almost certainty if you follow four specific rules.

Rule 1: Be Intelligent. It sounds unfair since intelligence is somewhat determined beyond our control—Genetics and our environment in early childhood are determinative. True, but be confident about your intelligence and sharpen it at every opportunity.

Rule 2: Be Knowledgeable. Education plays its role; however, only fools leave their education up to others, particularly the state (e.g., public schools). It is far less about what you learn in school than what you can avail yourself of outside school.

Most get the public dole-out of education. What sets one apart is what one obtains on their own.

Rule 3: Work Early, work hard. I once read a study describing the differences between American millionaires and non-millionaires. The only real difference between the two was what time of day they went to work, for both groups, on average, ended their day simultaneously.

The millionaires began their day on average 2 hours earlier, ending their day with all the other people, resulting in another mantra of mine, "Two hours earlier—ten hours more." John Ray, Benjamin Franklin, and many others said best: "The early bird catches the worm." The same thing is true with all investments—the earlier in life you invest, the greater your reward by retirement. Whatever you invest between the ages of 22 and 28—after accrued interest will be close to what you will have from 28 to 65—6 years vs. 37 years.

Work Hard. There is no substitute for putting sweat equity in your life. Showing up is essential, but what you accomplish while working makes a difference. Working too much can be worse than not working enough. At some point, the Law of Diminishing returns kicks in—you get less productivity for the time spent.

After the Law of Diminishing Returns, if you are not careful, you will arrive at the Law of Negative Returns. That's where you pay someone to work for you because you are so tired you screw up and break something that costs more than you made on the job.

If you start to work earlier than others, it gives you an automatic jump on the day. You don't waste time in rush hour. You receive the earlier stock tips, etc. The quality, quantity, and time you start work will help determine your success.

Rule 4: Ah. This is the all-important one. None of the rest matters without this one. (Drum Roll Please). Make good choices, and your relationship with the

Creator makes a difference, for according to Proverbs, the fear of the LORD is the foundation of knowledge and wisdom. A building with a firm foundation will succeed. If you understand its meaning, something makes sense, and you can't know its purpose without knowing the Creator. Finding that foundation of knowledge and wisdom allows for good decisions. It all begins and ends with Him.

Johannes Kepler, the great astronomer and mathematician, once wrote he was merely "thinking God's thoughts after Him." People more intelligent than me figured it out a long time ago. When we discover something, the Creator thought of it first. A brilliant person, like Kepler, realizes God has things figured out well, and maybe we should do things His way.

Me? I am more like the boy in the story who had been told not to play on the barn's metal roof because it is dangerous. As the boy slides down, he throws up a quick prayer, "Lord save me!" A nail catches him by his pants as he goes over the edge. "Never mind, Lord. I don't need you. The nail saved me." After everything I had been through, I always thought my ideas were better. Yes, even better than God's. My way of doing things was God gave me opportunities, and I took off on my own. That is the cusp of problems in my life. My life meets God's plan, and I go off without it.

My life was improving by incremental steps. I was making better choices. I had my children almost every weekend, progressing from Spring to Summer. It was good. We developed a routine. A consistent part of our routine was skating on Friday nights.

I noticed a Spelding County Deputy who worked at the skating rink most Friday nights—Greg Clerke. I knew him because he was the last officer to arrest me on Driving While License Suspended charges a few years before at the skating rink. One of the things that had fallen by the wayside of my drug-infused life was my driver's license. With Dad's help, I corrected the situation three years previously. Greg was a stickler for following the rules, which made him a jerk to me. I still think of him a little that way but with much less animus.

I had come to like and trust Greg through seeing him at the skating rink and engaging in conversation with him. He was a cop, but everybody had some bad characteristics.

At any rate, back to the story.

My phone rang. I didn't recognize the number. I answered. It was my young friend. An immediate flood of emotions washed through me—most were compassionate.

I know what you're thinking. The dude had aimed a loaded weapon at my face. I loved him. I loved him because he was my best friend's son. I loved him because I remembered who he was—deep beneath the surface and almost gone, nonetheless there. I had compassion for him because my heavenly Father had placed it in my heart. He wanted to apologize—an unheard-of thing for my young friend. We talked for a second, and we hung up. I knew the apology was sincere. I heard it in his voice, but I also knew he must be highly motivated, and I could not help him without some plan or backup.

I waited until Friday night. I approached Greg. "Well, David," Greg said, "You gotta know we want him, and when we catch him, because he'll be a four-time loser, it'll be life without the possibility of parole." Recidivism. That was what they would pin on him. I could not let it happen.

"What if I helped you get him? Can we use my efforts to buy a different sentence for him because that is what I have to offer? I help you all, and you make sure he gets rehab and is not sentenced to life without the possibility. Then, at least, maybe he'll have a shot at the rest of his life."

With a hopeful lilt, Greg replied, "Some will be up to him, and he'll do some time, but the rehab, without question, can be part."

We struck the deal. Enter Super Dave, with a giant S.D. on my imaginary tights, with the super-power of obstinate persistence.

"Since I spend most of my work week in Atlanta with the D.E.A., I'll have someone from Special Operations call you," Greg told me.

I waited. I waited for two weeks for the call to come. I am glad it took a minute for them to call. I had not thought this through very well. That was not unusual for me. I often operated from impulse to impulse. I needed to consider the consequences. I needed a plan. I needed to ensure I would come out of this as close to unscathed as possible.

The consequences were the apparent danger of dealing with people who have lost touch with morality and reality. Let's face it; it was not only the "gun in my face" incident; we read daily in the paper and see the news on T.V. of some drug deal gone wrong—warfare between gangs—and in the meth world, anything goes.

I am not a scaredy kind of guy. I'm also not "Super-Bad." I can handle myself but usually handle "situations" by talking the other person down. I'm not a fighter—if I can help it. Safety—my safety—was critical to me. I would need to be careful; however, being visibly cautious is not being careful. I would have to play a role, and circumstances, in large part, would determine it. I would have to be ready to roll with the punches—so to speak—and hopefully not actual punches.

Consequently, it was not only the drug world giving me fear. My last arrest had been on drug possession charges.

A reminder:

A Griffin Police Lieutenant pulled me over after purchasing cocaine. He asked to search my car. I, within my rights, refused. He yelled to another officer, "Call for a K-9 unit." I responded without hesitation, "That is illegal. If you do not pull me over with the K-9 unit, you cannot detain me while you wait for one." He responded, "Your right. Some recent case law has agreed with you, but you can complain about it later." After a while, the K-9 unit showed up, and still, the dog never alerted on anything. They searched my car anyway. The judge was complicit by refusing to give me a bond. My quickest way out was to accept the plea. It had been crystal clear Spelding County would "drag" me and hold me for a couple of years until it came up for trial.

Morality cannot be one-sided. What is good for the goose must be good for the gander.

So, I knew the police were unhesitant about breaking the law. The danger was real, but my young friend was worth the risk—and I trusted mister rule stickler Greg.

I needed a plan. That was simple. My young friend's inability to not gamble his money away left him in constant need of transportation—and I had it. I might also get by without using, but I am no fool, and if presented with a cause while playing a role, I'd use or fake use if possible—whatever I had to do. While I might like part of it, the toxic feeling after using was not worth it to me, or so I told myself. This was going to be quick and painless, anyway.

Quick and painless was important. I had finished my dad's remodel and worked at a local hotel during the day. While I do not require much sleep, I am not superhuman. I have only slept about 4 hours a night since I was 18, and working all day and driving all night for a week or two was only practical because work usually began at about 11 a.m., leaving me time for rest.

Essentially, I had concluded, not unusual for me, that to come out of this, it was all or nothing. Half-steps weren't feasible. I had to be the typical meth addict—if not in reality, in actions. I had seen enough of what it would take to model a meth addict.

Every drug brings out something different in individuals. With heroin, you have the nodders ("nodding" out or going to sleep). With crack comes almost uncontrollable facial tics. With meth, there's stupidity and paranoia. So, on the one hand, it would be easy to keep people off my scent by appearing stupid, playing on their paranoia, and keeping them looking at everybody else rather than me.

If I was clever with what I did, if I played well the role not yet determined, and if I ensured I had police permission to take some actions, I would walk out of this okay. The last thing was essential. But, again, I am not a complete fool. I would not be in trouble so long as the police were implicated in anything I did because I would most certainly be breaking some laws.

Of course, working for the police, even voluntarily, does not permit you to break the law, but they do it all the time. All I needed to do was ensure the police would be drawn into a scandal if they flipped on me. They are the ones who charge someone with a crime. A dangerous game, but one I could play. The same law that covers undercover law enforcement officers in challenging situations would protect me. If I felt my life was in danger, short of murder, getting away with almost anything was achievable. And, they could not compel me to testify against myself. There would be no cameras or recording devices—at my insistence. I was not bulletproof, but I had some covering. Besides, this was going to be quick and painless.

April 11—8:00 p.m.

Rest is good. The stress is not. My heart is racing too fast for me to count, and my chest hurts. No medicine and no help is coming. I have banged on the door. The intercom does not work.

I supposed if I got tangled up in this county, I'd be in a real fix. My assumption was not incorrect.

I need to lay still and breathe deeply-try calming down. Others have told me that dying in this jail is all too easy. Almost anywhere but here would be preferable.

I could try praying, but I think even God is tired of my crap. I wouldn't listen if I were Him.

I've tried calling anyone I could, but I don't have my phone, and the only numbers I remember are Greg's—I spoke with him; Dan's—I talked with him without much promise; Tim's—left him a message, but sure he won't respond; and Dad's—and he's not taking my calls.

There's still no warrant.

Alright, heart, keep on beating for the time being. Don't stop now!

11

Punched Down and Proofed Again

"This is Victor C." The phone call had finally come. "I will be handling you in your role as a confidential informant." I responded, "I have yet to contact my friend, but I believe he'll bite. He needs transportation badly." We discussed my role with the sheriff's department. Then he brought up my felony probation. "I'll have to get approval from your probation officer for you to do anything with us. Let me make that call, and I'll get back to you." A little more breathing room appeared. It turned into a couple more weeks of breathing room.

It was not a welcome couple of weeks' breathing room. Conflicted emotions? Law enforcement had been my enemy, to say the least. They had broken several laws, allowing for an illegal arrest, costing me a year of my life and guardianship of my children. (Whether rationalized or not, my mother taught me two wrongs do not make a right, and the cops were way past two). So, we decidedly had two different motivations. However, they could "snatch" my friend, Vick, out of the fire, which I had proven myself incapable of—partly due to my addiction issues and how far my friend had slipped. It was going to require a massive effort.

My motivation? I wanted Vick back. Nobody in the drug world called him by his given name. Most didn't know his name. So, instead, he went by the nom de guerre of "Mustang." The nickname went back to his teen years when he first started dealing because he drove a Ford Mustang. My friend operated on two different frequencies. Now and then, Vick would show up, but more and more these days, Mustang, his dark twin, dominated his psyche.

Vick is kind and caring. He will go out of his way to be pleasant and agreeable. One time, a couple of years back, I got a call from him. He was so excited; he almost effervesced through the phone line. "David, are you still looking for work?" I replied, "I am always looking for work." "You have helped me with work, and I finally can get you back." He told me about his new job and said they were still hiring. He and I would be partners servicing air conditioners at hotels nationwide. It was to be one of the best jobs I have ever had. He, however, lasted about two months because of the living chemistry set he had become. I stayed until the broken coccyx and illegal arrest.

Then there is Mustang—the cut-throat, dishonest, lying, and thieving individual who had assumed my young friend's body, and a clear line of demarcation existed between the two so severe that I have often wondered about the veracity of multiple personality disorder and if Vick possessed it. Mustang is the kind of person who will continue to lie to you even when you know he is lying because it is the evil thing to do. He is irresponsible and unable to keep a job, much less a relationship. Mustang would never call me about a job unless he intended to steal my paycheck.

The cops' motivation? That was clear. They did not like him, and it wasn't so much about enforcing the law as it was doing the job of making arrests—not so much about ridding the community of the plague of meth. The long and short of it was Mustang had ticked them off too many times, so it had become personal. Even though I was somewhat jaded, my total disenfranchisement would not come until later. I believed law and order was at least part of their motivation. Some good officers care. I've met them. It was not in the cards for me to work with any of those in the coming year—with perhaps the exception of my "rule-stickler" friend Greg. Perhaps I am being unfair to officers like Victor C. Maybe their hands were tied somewhat; perhaps they had become jaded—maybe they didn't know what to do or whether to trust someone who volunteered to do what I did. Perhaps they did not understand the love for my best friend's son motivating me to extravagance.

While I understood we were approaching my friend from two polar opposites, I was unconcerned about their motivations. I only cared that Vick got help before he hurt someone or himself. I loved—they didn't. They had the power necessary to help—I didn't. "The enemy of my enemy is my friend" did not even apply here, for Vick was not my enemy, but we shared a common solution, and they had promised to be somewhat lenient.

Now we return to the all-important question, "Who in their right mind…?" I had to pose the healing of my relationship with my young friend so he would accept it without question. I have often said, "I am the smartest idiot you'll ever meet." Being as gifted as I am and making choices like I do doesn't make sense.

However, sometimes I do the things I do for my reasons—reasons that don't jibe with other people. I might appear an idiot at those times, but I am not—just otherwise motivated. This was one of those times. I needed to be the kind of person who took what my friend said: hook, line, and sinker. I had to appear to fall for his con. It was hard for me to swallow, but again, this would be quick and painless.

I've said that before, haven't I?

Victor C. called after two weeks, saying they had approval from my probation officer. It was the first of many lies to come.

I called my young friend. We made a deal. Thus began my journey into the rabbit hole—as it were. I called Victor C. and let him know. The plan was simple. I would touch base with Victor C. whenever my friend called for a ride. I would give him all the information, and they would, in turn, figure out a way to arrest Vick without endangering me. One of the biggest problems, Mr. C. said, was that Vick stayed in a different hotel every day and stayed on the road all night. They also wanted to make sure the arrest counted. In other words, Vick needed to have a decent quantity of dope on him.

The calls from Vick came daily. I was patient. Special Operations was trying to find the best way to work this out. I talked with or texted Victor C. daily.

Here, I should pause for a quick note. Are you having trouble separating Vick from Victor C.? You're not the only one! I had saved Vick's name in my phone as Vick. It was not a problem because I did not keep Victor C.'s number, for I memorized it after almost confusing one for the other on a phone call. Their phone numbers were virtually identical, which complicated matters further. The first six numbers were 678-588 for both of them. The last four were, and these are representatives—not the real ones—9805 and 5809. I do not exaggerate. What are the odds their names would be the same and their numbers have the same ten digits, almost in the same order? It was to present a problem later on. I have made things a little less confusing by calling my best friend's son, Vick, and my handler, Victor C. It was indeed an opportunity for confusion!

So, I had roles to play. First was to Spelding County—keeping open and honest communication with my handler—always covering my butt by complying with what they wanted, no less, no more. Then, I had to play a role at work–working with no rest but doing my best, remaining optimistic, and treating my boss and customers with the utmost respect. Finally, I had a role to play as a parent—my employment served me well for supporting my children in what they wanted to do with me after driving two hours to pick them up! As their parent, child support was paid dutifully by my father from my pay for work completed on his house.

I also had a role to play in my spiritual life—that role almost immediately took a back seat to everything else. Reading what I am writing now helps me understand the pressures I had placed on myself—forces I ignored because I could push on through anything in my life by sheer strength of will—at least, I convinced myself.

And I had the "intelligent idiot and easily manipulated" role for Vick and his friends. For my safety, I had to play this one to the hilt. It was not too difficult. If there is a drug that makes you more stupid than methamphetamine, I don't know what it is. Since almost all meth dealers use their supply, you should get the point. Again, it's not difficult, but doing anything well takes concentration and persistence, and being good at it 99% of the time wasn't good enough. I had to be perfect. One lapse could be catastrophic—e.g., the hospital or the grave.

Most people play multiple roles in their lives. At one moment, a man is a lover to his wife. At another, he is a father to a young child. If he has several children, he may have to be the confidant of a teenager in love within moments of consoling a young child over a skinned knee. Then, after doing all of that, he has to pick up the car keys and head to work where his role is entirely different—not to mention how he acts or performs in the bowling league, social club, or church. These roles are consistent with each other. Yes, they are different roles, but they all complement each other. My problem, as with an average undercover officer, was that I had to be two different kinds of people. One on the inside—one on the outside. One sometimes and the polar opposite at another. It is easy to do for a few minutes. Holding on to your sanity for two weeks is much more challenging but not impossible. Extend it much more, and maintaining your cover and mind becomes more extravagantly harder each day. What was promised to me by my handler and his bosses was to be a two-week, at the most, operation. That would give them enough time to sort out the difficulties, make the arrest, and keep a lid on Vick until they could get him into rehab through jail.

Part of the difficulty of living with such a split personality was not just trying to stay out of trouble but realizing I had to burn bridges in the process. People might take notice. If they tagged me mentally with my young friend, gossip around town, in church, and the family would abound. Gossip is no one's friend.

I had to come to grips with sacrificing some relationships for Vick. Nobody else would save him. As I have said, I was the last man standing. While I might be internally burning up with regret, it had to appear as user angst. I did not deeply consider many factors at this point. How much of this would matter since I would be working through the night in a vehicle, playing my role, when most sane people are sawing logs? It wasn't for very long.

It was a risk, but not a serious one. Besides, from the beginning, I was the only one who took my role seriously. I was the only one who thought about my risks. I was the only one who thought the sheriff's department cared enough to tell the truth and ensure they followed through on what they said.

I must stop and address the apparent lack of spiritual walk in my life then. That role had fallen by the wayside. I had a relationship with my heavenly Father, but it was more like teenagers' relationship with their parents. "Hey, Dad. I love you. Can I have the car keys?" but then he walks away and forgets who his parent is. The problem is while I knew Him, I had yet to spend enough quality time with Him—to fall in love with Him. My heart and spirit were open to Him on my later road north because I had nothing left to occupy my mind. I had no choice—no real choice, that is. I could have done something different, but I had come to a place of complete surrender because nothing else valid was left to me. He wants everyone there—not because He is a control freak but because He wants us to reach for and have a happy, successful life. We can only achieve abundant life by living out our purpose.

The following is something God gave me the morning I wrote this chapter.

Perhaps it will help you understand (from the Baker and the Bread on Facebook, 6/25/2018):

"Dave's Double Dose

The past couple of "Doses" have led me to contemplate a subject. We are so quick to judge others, but from what standard do we pass judgment?

We human beings have something broken in us. Our makeup, environment, and genes lead us to operate in a self-motivated fashion. Most of us are geared to care about others. That comes from a combination of spiritual motivation hanging on from before "The Fall" of Adam, current input from God, and self-preservation, for we hope to gain something by doing for others.

But our wisdom is much like using a wheelbarrow to move a load of bricks across town when a truck and forklift are available—it sort of works. It eventually arrives at a place that appears successful. The bricks are moved. Some are broken. Some are lost. You can still build the house, but different from the one you were meant to have. However, you are now exhausted, and you still have a lot of work to do.

Through our ignorance and experimental living, we accept a set of deceptively errant rules because they do achieve something. However, God created this universe with a different set of Laws. Those Laws are not based on what we do but on who He is. Now, we can circumvent those Laws and sometimes find something we want, but we still can't discover the thing for which we are genuinely searching.

Joy, peace, happiness, and prosperity. We all crave these things. There is only one Law that will provide those things. Live out your purpose—have a relationship with your Creator. Do that, and "all these things shall be added unto you."

You say, "What? It can't be that simple."

I am afraid it is. There should be no great effort on our part. He does all the heavy lifting. When we try to achieve without him, we lose our bricks. They break. And we become exhausted. We never are satisfied with the results, and "all these things" elude us.

He gives us more than hints we are operating with the wrong rules. Tithe and the windows of heaven will pour out so many blessings we cannot handle them all. The last shall be first. Serve, for in serving, we become leaders. The list goes on and on. We sometimes grasp part of the message and then corrupt it with our broken wisdom. We serve because serving teaches us something that makes us better leaders. While it may be so, serving with being a leader as the end goal ruins the beauty and pleasure of service.

I'll close with this. We have been duped, confused, and misused by society, our predecessors, and ourselves. Throw out your concepts of what works. You're mistaken. Create a clean slate God can use on which to write. Seek Him first. That's where you'll find success. Anything else is a lie and will give you only a counterfeit of success.

What is the most significant Law you need to discover? The Law of Grace. You need to find out how it applies to you and how to implement Grace to others.

To discover that, you need to talk to our Father.

He is awaiting your call.

In Christ Alone,
the Bread
(A Product of the Loving Baker)

Let's get back to my wheelbarrows and role-playing situation.

I did not consider any of this to be a problem. Law enforcement sure did not have a problem arresting me a year and a half before, nor did they have trouble keeping me in jail without a bond. Surely, if they could do that to me, they would put a lid on Vick. He may sober up long enough to start looking up to where the answer is. Maybe he would figure out no life was in what he was doing. Maybe he would see how many people he was hurting. Maybe I could, for once, be a part of a positive solution for someone—even if nobody ever knew—a lot of maybe's. Maybe one would work.

Maybe.

April 13—5:00 p.m.

Who needs a warrant? Well, technically, they have one. Spelding County didn't issue one, but that didn't stop Mick Marr. They zipped a judge in here a few minutes ago. Without probable cause given from where my "crime" took place, they have charged me with possession of stolen property—a property that has not been reported stolen by the relevant jurisdiction.

I guess Mick is finally getting his revenge from years ago. I'm trapped in his jail. No medication and no help from outside—well, maybe Greg. After all, there was no warrant. I wonder how long Mick'll be able to keep this up.

I'll be dressed out and put in the back of the General population. Then, if I start having chest pains again, I'll be around others. At least someone will be there if I die the next time.

I called Greg—no answer—I left him a long message.

12

Greased Pan

It did not take me long to end up with a nickname. Vick often shortened his reference to me from Uncle David to "Unk." So he would introduce me as Uncle David and turn around and call me Unk.

The abbreviation began to stick. At first, I was not overly fond of it, but then it started being an affectionate term. Not many people knew my real name. Both of those things were good things. These people were addicts. I cared about them. I wanted them out of "the life." Gaining an affectionate title meant I hoped they would listen to things I might say one day. In the beginning, my goal was to get in and get out. The longer I stayed in, the more people I met, the more I might impact these people. The addicts were never my target for legal difficulties. I was at odds with law enforcement, but I didn't care.

Victor C. called, "David, things have just been crazy. I've been so busy. Simply put, we need more time. We haven't been able to put together a good plan."

The two-week plan had already become three weeks. Exhaustion set in. I said I understood. I didn't. It seemed impossible that they could not conceive of a way to make a bust. Vick rarely had a considerable quantity on him. Between his and his entourage's drug use and his penchant for gambling on the "ching" machines, he seemed only to be able to scrape enough money together to buy an ounce at a time—but an ounce was plenty. Nevertheless, it is true that finding a way to make the arrest and avoid an entanglement involving me was decidedly tricky.

While Vick would only purchase an ounce of meth at a time, we made two or three trips on some nights to South Atlanta, East Atlanta, Fayetteville, Jonesboro, or Stockbridge. Victor C. always had a reason they couldn't arrest him. Usually, it was too late. In my few conversations with "Mr. Rules" Greg, he cautioned me that if I was stopped outside Spelding County, I might very well be in trouble myself; Victor C. assured me they would cover me. I was, according to him, working under their umbrella. Because of my agreement with law enforcement, Vick traveling without me, for Vick's sake, was not something I wanted. I was sure they'd get him; if I sat on the sidelines, he would end up with a life sentence.

So, drive I did—night after grueling night. Every day was a new reason given by Spelding County Special Operations. "Not enough people on staff." "Not the right people on duty."

I continued. I was developing a relationship with Victor C. He seemed like a nice enough guy. Though I know he lied to me occasionally, I still believe he was reasonably honest. I was sure the interference in wrapping things up came from above him.

All the information about where we went and who Vick saw outside the county was funneled directly to

Greg. He was the D.E.A. guy, though employed by Spelding County. I began to notice a trend. Within a couple of weeks of my young friend seeing a particular weight dealer (someone who sold large quantities at a time), law enforcement popped the dealer—by local agencies, sometimes by the D.E.A., and occasionally by The G.B.I., but the D.E.A. was almost always involved. Now, I am absolutely sure those dealers were already on somebody's radar, but it became enough of a pattern that I greatly suspect they were using my information. I was okay with that. It's why I gave it to them, and they got a wealth of it from me. Why would they not at least say, "Hey, Dave? Good job on that one. That was righteous info." Or something similar? There are several possibilities I will ponder about later in this story.

Approximately six weeks into this adventure, Victor C said they had a plan. I would drive into the same RaceTrac station this book will reach later and go into the store. They would arrest Vick in the parking lot. I would be close to the situation, but I almost didn't care by this point. I was beyond exhausted. Working all day, being a Dad in the afternoon and evening, and driving all night was more than taking a toll on my constitution.

The truth is I was angry.

I wasn't only angry at the law enforcement officers; I was near the point of rage at my young friend, but I still had a role to play with Vick. I would calmly discuss the things that angered me, but on the inside, I was seething.

You must remember I am the father of five; four are girls. My number one problem? His objectification of women. I know the psychology of it all. Deep inside, he abhorred himself and sought to fill that emptiness with outward affection. But, of course, we aren't made to be a ship in any port, so to cover the lack of relationships in misguided sexual exploits, we objectify sexual partners. These girls were walking into it with eyes wide shut. He was cool. He was a drug dealer. He said he loved them, and of course, he had a steady supply of drugs.

In the same vein, no woman with any self-respect left wants to be considered a whore or a "dirty butt," as the colloquial expression goes, so they would play psychological tricks on themselves, lie to themselves, and say they had fallen in love with him.

Inevitably, he would tire of a particular side attraction within a few days and return to his main girlfriend. Invariably, within hours, a phone call from the latest girl came, "Unk? I hate him. I hate everything about him!" etc. I would listen, and my stock answer was always, "You had to know from the beginning you were nothing more than a side entertainment to him." It was a cold response delivered in a compassionate tone. As long as they lied to themselves, they would never accept a greater truth. The only way to avoid more pain, like what they were experiencing, was to get out of that life. The only time we stop using is when the pain of using becomes greater than the pain of not using. In a way, warped as it is, Vick may very well be a part of some of these young ladies' eventual recovery from addiction. The rest would spiral deeper.

One time, as the seething became so great I could not contain it, I nearly lost my cool at him over his treatment of these girls. His response was, "It's their fault. They know what they're doing." It matters not that what he said is true. We have a responsibility for how we treat others. We have a responsibility for what happens because of how we treat others. The very fact that I was living within this subset of humanity was based upon how he treated others—including me. It was also evidence I had taken a God thing to the other extreme. I was sacrificing good things in my life and good people to achieve what I believed to be a greater goal. I had become Machiavelli's Prince. I justified my actions for the greater good, much like the officer did during my previous arrest. I was no different. My justification? It was only for a couple of weeks, and I could recoup the damage later by fixing it. The problem? The more I was enmeshed in "the life," the more damage I was doing, and the harder it would be to fix.

Things were beginning to spiral out of my control, though. It was becoming evident the police were not going to move very fast. They had their agenda.

My role as an employee was suffering. I was too tired to perform at my best. Although the job did not pay well, my parents raised me always to do my best—no matter the pay. My best was my responsibility. The salary was the employer's. I kept the job because it provided perfect cover for me and gave me an alternate site to deal with Vick—other than my father's home. I still performed, though, and the owner liked me. It was at least working for me at the moment.

My, unmentioned before, role as a son to my father was faltering. I had stopped doing minor things to his house to finish all my work. I had not replaced all the vent covers or completed some woodwork on the back porch. I was too tired and preoccupied with completing this deal with the sheriff's department.

On Fridays, when my children were not in town, we went out to eat and to see a movie. My sister had started it with Dad and Mom when she moved back to town a few years earlier. It was important because they included me when I came home from rehab. I had not been invited before. I stopped going. I didn't have time. When my kids were home, they came first. I was always with them, but other significant things, like the movies, church, and prayer life, began to fall by the wayside.

I may have considered myself a Superman who could make things happen by sheer force of will, but I had more weaknesses than just Kryptonite. First, I needed rest—I wasn't getting nearly enough. I needed to eat right, and I needed some success in my life. However, when stretched to the breaking point, you cannot be successful in anything you do.

Besides this volunteer work for Vick/sheriff's department, the only thing I reserved strength for was my children, and up to this point, I had not failed them since I had been home.

When it came to the last two children I had left, I would pull out all the stops. If they wanted Six Flags—we had season passes—we went to Six Flags. If Paul or Grace had to go to camp, I made whatever extra trips it required. Once, I made six trips in one week, two hours away to Welsington, GA, to accommodate their summer schedules and make it to Six Flags, with two of those trips made in the middle of the night. They were essential to me, and, in my mind, they had suffered enough. They deserved me going out of my way. It would spoil some children. Mine? Okay, they were a little spoiled, but their grades stayed on track, as did their behavior. As long as that was true, the least I could do was jump over a few hurdles and through a few hoops. They were more important to me than anything else, but I had to finish what I had started.

"Okay, David. We have a plan." With those words, my anger almost dissipated.

Now, nervousness set in. On the one side of me, I wanted to make sure I did precisely what Victor C wanted me to do. It was an operation involving lots of moving parts. I wanted to make sure I did my part. I like to perform well. On another side of me was sorrow. After all, I hate seeing anybody go down, but if someone ever needed to get a grip, it was Vick, and this was his last hope—I believed.

On yet another side of me was fear. I had already met some pretty dangerous cats in this business. Would the sheriff's department pull this off without implicating me? This would finally be over, but would it mean the end of me? I had considered this might be a consequence of my actions—a slight chance, but possible. Dave's "Stress-O-Meter" was way in the red.

Fear of me failing in some way, fear Vick would find out I was involved, and I would never be able to reach him, fear others would find out and end me were all very real, all palpable.

I had a day to let it chew me up inside while I mulled over potential consequences—86,400 seconds, modified by fear, ticking in slow motion. You can talk about Einsteinian warped time and relativity theories all you want to, but I can tell you through personal experience how to modify time—fear. This was going down in 24 hours. I had no choice in the matter; I had to be ready.

A sleepless night passed, and I had gotten myself as ready as possible. I got the call from Vick. I went and picked him up. It was only him and me, no females or entourage for once. I pulled over.

"Vick. You've got to get out of this life. There's no future in it. If you could figure out a way to save the ton of money you make, I'd bankroll you and be all supportive—set a time frame, make some money, and get out. But you can't save any of the money. You use it up or gamble it away. You've got nothing and will end up in prison again or dead."

"I know, Unk. I know I am going back to prison. They just haven't caught me yet."

"Then why continue? It's foolishness, Vick; say the word, and I'll back out of this place. I'll aim the front of this car west and drive until the wheels get wet. We'll put our money together and make a new start in California or Oregon. Hell, maybe even Alaska. Somewhere a long way away where our pasts won't follow us."

"Uncle David, I wish I could. This is the only life I know."

"You know that's not true. We have worked together enough. I know you can do other things. You had a good job in South Georgia. That's a lie you're telling yourself. Get out and get out tonight! I have a bad feeling about things. Things may go bad for us if we don't pull out."

"Oh, I'm going back to prison if I stay here. I know it."

"Then let's just go."

I don't know how I would have handled things if he had agreed, but I would have backed out and headed west. I would have found an answer for the rest of my life. I would have been ecstatic; nothing would have stopped me from doing what I had proposed. There's no way I would have separated myself from my children forever. I would have found an answer to both. It's what went through my mind unnecessarily because Mustang interrupted my thoughts,

"Let's go. They're waiting on me."

I privately contacted Victor C. while Vick made a rather uncharacteristically large purchase of 3 ounces. Everything was in place back at the RaceTrac, according to Victor C. My young friend had a large enough quantity on him. It looked like everything was zooming in on the target.

"Pull over at the next gas station; I need a pack of cigarettes," ordered Vick, "and you need gas."

"I was going to stop at the RaceTrac, but okay."

I was not in a good enough position to argue. With heavy traffic, we were still 30 minutes from the RaceTrac, and his nicotine need would not wait that long. I went into the store to pay for gas and got his cigarettes. When I came back out, Vick was in the driver's seat. "I just got a call, and I can get rid of half this in one stop. I'm going to drive, though. We gotta go down 155. Pump the gas." From behind the car, I called Victor C to let him know the change of direction was out of my control but gave him our exact route and my release to stop my car and search it so they would have no difficulties. My nerves were beyond frayed. I wanted this over. I couldn't take anymore.

"I don't know if we can make the change. I'm calling it off." With that pronouncement, he crushed me. What kind of crap was this? I had built some trust for Victor C. What was going on? It was about the stupidest thing I had ever heard. They sure didn't have to do anything intricately impossible to pull me over when they arrested me. There was nothing I could do. So I put back on my cover and called my son to cover why I was on the phone. I was talking to him when I got back in the car.

Also, with the pronouncement, Spelding County Special Operations knowingly allowed three ounces of Crystal Methamphetamine to be distributed on the streets they should have stopped. With the six to eight weeks prior of at least an ounce a day, they could have stopped fifty-plus ounces. So now fifty-three ounces of destruction, fifty-three ounces of young men and women brain-destroying, mind and life-warping chemicals were allowed on the streets of my community. They could have stopped it. They didn't. Of course, I had taken the typical long view. It would take effort, and it is not as easy to make a clean arrest as one might presume, and my young friend would not cop a plea. A clean bust was a necessity. But this? Long view or not, this was over the top for me. It was beyond reason. I did not have an answer, and later, when I probed Victor C., I was given more excuses.

My complete disenfranchisement had begun. Now, there was only one reason for what I was doing-Saving Vick—snatching him out of the fire in which he willingly stood, although compelled by his addiction, had walked into and was steadily being burned. But, just as steadily, he spread the wildfire around, destroying other precious lives. I could stay involved, close this up, and try to make a difference.

But now? What about next Tuesday? And that one reason? It would soon expand to two more!

April 17

The chest pains and shortness of breath returned—last night? The night before? I don't remember. The past many hours are running together in my head. When the pain returned, the jail guards had some inmates drag me out of the cell block on my mat and into a holding cell. They locked the door and turned out the light, apparently waiting for me to die. I didn't oblige them.

Still no meds. Still no doctor. When I didn't kick the bucket, they returned me to another cell block.

If I had no other reason to survive, it is the hope of someday rubbing this in the face of the unrepentant sheriff and his wife—my ex-wife.

That day will come. Greg will not stand by and do nothing. He was so disgusted by Spelding County's mistreatment of me that he threatened to quit. Either he's an excellent liar, or he's very sincere. I am left with nothing but hope the latter is true.

13

Pre-shaped

Despite the sheriff's department's indecisiveness and inability to understand what their inaction was doing to me, things were still moving in a somewhat positive direction for me in my personal life—well, what personal life I had.

My probation officer liked me. I had never failed a drug screen. I had a decent relationship with her, and then him who came after her. I passed all the visits from the probation department to my home with flying colors.

While I failed to finish some small items in remodeling Dad's house, he had proclaimed it an outstanding job—even if he was a little frustrated with me.

To help explain what appeared to anyone as erratic behavior, I broke down and told him about my work with the sheriff's department and its connection to the DEA through Greg, whom Dad also knew. He didn't like it, but with assurances from me that it would be short-lived, he accepted it.

My relationship with my two youngest continued to grow stronger. Every weekend visit during the previous school year had turned into spending much of the summer together. We made multiple trips to Six Flags and Whitewater. We played. We did the skating rink thing every Friday night. I would skate a little with my youngest and shoot a little pool with my son (a game my son plays all too well).

Of course, my children's persistent presence added a whole other dimension. Now, I would work all day, spend all evening with my children, put them to bed, and drive most of the night for Vick. It was insanity at its finest, and there is no doubt about the wear and tear it was putting on my life.

Despite this, Dad and I had put a plan into motion to get my children and me back under the same roof. I had done almost everything the juvenile court required to return guardianship to me. I only needed a psychological profile from the Department of Family and Children's Services.

However, Fall was approaching, and Dad and I wanted them back in Griffin for the start of the school year. To this end, we made many preparations.

My son would be in high school. My youngest would be starting middle school. It was my youngest child's situation that concerned me. The Middle School had changed administrator hands.

It had been excellent when their older sister had attended the same school. But then, the school's leadership staff and the student body's makeup changed. My son had fared well into the 7th grade, but things were in a tailspin.

Almost weekly, stories appeared in the paper about the school—gang activity, drug busts, and the like were becoming too commonplace. In an attempt to clamp down on the student body, the school was spending far too much time marching in the halls, practicing rudimentary social skills, and far too little time hitting the books.

I had investigated every private school around. Dad had first vocalized my concerns about the school situation and agreed with my analysis. He offered to foot the bill for whichever school I deemed the best answer for Grace.

Interestingly enough, the Flint River Baptist Camp where Mom had so selflessly served for many years had been sold to a private concern and converted into a private school. Much of the purchase funds had come from a grant by Truitt Cathy—the founder of Chick-fil-A. The school was doing well, and I felt I was the best place suitable for my daughter.

Mid-summer brought disappointment for me. Paul was in his mid-teen years—a sensitive time at best. He expressed his desire to stay in Welsington, where he had made a new set of friends. With all the upheaval I had caused in his life, I was not about to force the issue. He was at the point where many decisions would have to be his. I encouraged my teenagers to make decisions with my guidance, but they must also accept responsibility for their choices. We discussed. He knew I disagreed, but I would support him in whatever he did—so long as it was well thought out and moving in a positive direction. I was still his Dad; it must be from a distance.

I was down to my last child, Grace, who would be in my care.

****

Writing a memoir is, I'm sure, a lot different from, say, a novel. In fiction, one must think about the plot, devise the twists and turns of the story, and invent people. I'm sure that is a painstaking process. I have yet to find out. I've never done it. So, I don't know what a novelist or writer goes through when writing.

I am not a novelist, and other writers worldwide are likely glad to hear me say I'm not like them.

This is not a novel. I wrote Most of this story in May, June, and July 2018. I froze when I got to the final line of the last chapter about the following Tuesday. It is not writer's block. I haven't suddenly lost the ability to write; I have posted over 400 blogs amounting to 400k+ words since then.

It is fear.

At this point, I had already begun to push the envelope. I was living on the edge, but my fear was not of some of the people I encountered. They were dangerous, and some harmed me, but time has elapsed, and my faith and walk with Christ have removed most of the fear. Time may heal, but I serve the greatest Healer, and He is also my Protector. So, no, my fear is not of evil people. They hold no power over me anymore.

My fear is not for people I knew either. A good number of them have found sobriety and now follow my blog. Their lives are no longer my responsibility. If they are still in "the life," I can only pray for them. If there are those in law enforcement who, either by design or in ignorance, seek to harm me, it is also in my Father's hands. I have learned to rely entirely on Him.

No, my fear is in the writing, for unlike a novel, I do not have to contrive a plot. Unlike a fictional account, I do not have to make up characters for my story. Unlike a novel, I do not write for pleasure.

I write to tell the story but to tell it, I must relive it.

The redemption that comes later is easy. While some might bring personal anguish and regret, my ancient memories from earlier life have receded from prominence in my mind. Even writing about my life on the edge was simple enough.

What happens next in my story remains a wound—oozing with potential infection. Over two years later, I had to change the spiritual bandages and apply more ointment of prayer. It broke something deep inside me, requiring a long time to heal. This part of my story changed everything, for after the events of the coming Tuesday, I made yet another choice. I was no longer living on the edge. I leaped into the chasm. I dove into Alice's rabbit hole, as it were. I had only one choice, one option ahead, and it was an all-or-nothing proposition.

There was no way I would come out unscathed, and a strong likelihood I might not make it out, but while I might have had other choices, they were all untenable.

This is not a novel. This is not fiction. I am not crafting a story. It was all too real, and as I write, I must dredge up memories, and in the process, I must relive them.

So, it is the writing I fear. The experiences were bad enough, and I lived in terror at points. My mistakes, and thus, my regret, must be felt all over again. But the hardest part? The great sadness reconstituting from memory seeks to pull my soul to the depths as if an anchor were tied about my waist while attempting to swim the world's oceans. So, I find myself, in the writing, stumbling about in the darkness all over again, devoid of hope, fearing my actions, in the end, would be pointless.

****

The day arrived. As I approached the day, I had no great sense of anxiousness. I had done all the necessary work. I had the youngest's school situation lined up. I had done everything. No one should be able to say anything too damaging. I had my probation officer's backing. Besides, this hearing was supposed to be a formality. My older daughter, who had guardianship, had vocalized support for Grace returning home with me. Everything was good.

Or so I thought.

The first sign I should have noticed was my ex-wife's attitude. There was nothing unusual about her attitude. She wanted others to view her favorably, but she commonly wanted to do something other than what she needed to achieve that. She haphazardly paid child support and didn't make time for the kids, but she didn't want to see me win—as she viewed it—ignoring that it wasn't about me winning; it was about what was best for our youngest.

We took the conversation outside.

"Look, it's relatively straightforward. This is a formality. If you try to insert garbage into this proceeding, I'll tell the judge the truth. You're behind thousands of dollars in child support to me and the same to Lydia, and you never see the kids, though nobody is stopping you. I have even facilitated you seeing them despite you many times. That's the unadulterated truth. Like it or not!"

"Stop trying to intimidate me. You're intimidating me!"

"Intimidating you with the truth? Perhaps you should examine your life."

Her ex-counselor husband yelled at me from the door, "You better stop intimidating her!" It must have been a prearranged script since he could not hear our conversation.

I went back inside, shaking my head, but I should have realized that with a prearranged script, something was afoot.

The crowd in the court waiting room seemed to grow larger. People who had no direct reason for being there were beginning to arrive. It should have made me nervous. Not perceiving made what was to come so much more surprising.

Sucker-punch: "A true sucker punch is quite a bit more complex than a simple unannounced attack. It primarily involves a closed fist contacting the soft underbelly of a person, … (which) leaves the victim open to various other attacks. (UrbanDictionary.com)

I had assumed others had been honest with me; an assumption, combined with exhaustion from my current extracurricular efforts, left me with my guard down. Believing this to be a formality, I had already lost before the day began.

The clerk called my case, and everyone filed into the courtroom. The sucker punch landed almost immediately.

"I'm Judge ****. Does anyone have any questions before we get started?"

I don't remember what my question was going to be, oh, but I do remember the judge's response to my raised hand.

"You, sir, don't open your mouth in my courtroom!"

I was not the only one who had filled out paperwork before the day. It was clear who was responsible for directing the blow—my daughter, L, who then used the bulk of the time tearing into me and whose attacks went unabated by the judge. Yes, the person who had proclaimed her support to my face had delivered the blow.

I do not know who she had managed to convince to write the court against me, but I have figured some of it out. Whoever wrote, it doesn't matter. The damage was done. I had already been shut down in my own hearing, and this was the juvenile court where the judge is the potentate. This king exercises his authority without due process and on his whim. I did not get to face my accusers or even find out the accusations. I had no opportunity to offer a defense. I was proverbially hauled out and lynched.

The blow had been deadly to me. In no uncertain terms, the judge told me I would never have my children again.

While I would never wish evil on anyone, had I not already run off and started doing what God had laid out for me to do on my own, had I been standing firmly in my faith, I would have seen God's hand at work beginning immediately after that farce of a hearing. Still, I had left God's path and wasn't standing on a firm foundation.

Instead, I was left demolished, crushed, defeated, and looking for solutions alone; I took the plunge. Instead, I missed everything God did. What happened in court was ugly, and as a friend once said, "God doesn't like ugly!"

For those who did the wrong thing, their lives spun into disaster and chaos. I'm under no illusions I'm different from God's other children. When He adopts us into his family, He takes care of us—in blessings, discipline, and revenge (vengeance is never our call to make). I have been on the receiving end of it all.

Had I been the least bit plugged into my Heavenly Father, I would have seen His swift action as the house of cards in my opponents' lives began to crumble. But, instead, I missed it all. I was too wrapped up in myself, and I missed learning something I have since learned, for in spinning off even further on my own, the chaos that would ensue in my life would leave me with no choices, as you will soon discover.

The first one was arrested at the courtroom door for an obscure warrant from years before and spent months in jail. Jobs were lost. Psychological problems went into full bloom, and financial ruin threatened a few. And I do not make light of it. Nevertheless, it would have been better if we had done the right thing.

Regrettably, not one did—including me.

Devastated, I crossed the parking lot to my vehicle and got in. I sat as my mind roiled in dismay and confusion. The work I had been doing had played a part in my destruction. Nobody knew. Nobody could know. However, if I had any hope of ever countering what went on in court, it would be me proving I had contributed something positive to my community, thereby gaining the endorsement of law enforcement.

It was no longer simply about my young friend, Vick. That was my primary goal, but I would have to cast my net wider. The sheriff's department had already offered to pay me, and the DEA proposed a similar arrangement, but I had turned it all down.

They continued to say many things. I would continue to turn money down, but I clung to one promise. They committed to expunge my record because I had gone above and beyond, and in the process, I hoped to gain favor with the juvenile court.

It may seem convoluted to you, but I saw no other options. So, I decided in the middle of the parking lot of the Juvenile Court on Solomon Street. I would do whatever it took. I would be willing to do anything.

I would have to be viewed as a hero to the good guys, but there was only one way I could obtain the information I needed. I would have to get my hands dirtier and go deeper than what I had been going, and I got the blessings of Victor C.

"If you're in the county, it'll be no problem. I'll make sure charges are never filed if you're picked up, and if you're outside the county, you might have to sit in jail for a few hours until I can pick you up. We have a good relationship with all the surrounding counties, so you'll be alright."

I'm not stupid. I didn't trust law enforcement any more than the drug dealers. I figured Victor C. was good for his word, but I knew he had limits despite what he said. Again, though, I would have nothing to worry about as long as I produced.

I drove home angry and frustrated. Then I called my control officer, Victor C., and Vick, with the same message to both.

"I'm outta court. Let's do this thing!"

April 18

Well, that didn't take long. The deputies came in, had me dress back into my clothes, and informed me Spelding County was on its way to get me. All charges in Moore County were magically dropped. Imagine that!

The ride to Spelding County was incredible. When prompted, the transport officer was a Christian who did not mind sharing his faith. And the music! I felt like God was trying to speak to me through this mess. I don't understand why He would, but I felt like I went to church for the first time in a long time. It felt soul-cleansing—almost.

I had hoped this was a courtesy ride back to Spelding because these charges would be disappeared, but nope. We will see what happens. Being in this jail, where I participated in many incarcerations, did not leave me feeling very comfortable.

I have no idea where the attempts on my life have come from. Supposedly, the cops know, but I do wonder which ones? And can I trust them?

14

Let It Rise

Go in deeper, make as big of a dent in the methamphetamine business as possible, and get out alive. That's what "doing this thing" meant to me.

Make lots of money and show everybody who the true "playa" was; it's what I wanted Vick and others to believe.

Getting my young friend off the street and wiping out the drug trade, at least in Spelding County, was what team Dave and Spelding County was supposed to be all about, according to Victor C.

However, something wasn't adding up.

How long do you need to keep someone on the inside to have what information you need to pull someone over—when you know when and where they were?

My opinion wavered between complete incompetence on the authorities' parts to somehow crookedly protecting the drug trade to a desire to use me to make as many busts as possible—at the cost of hampering the drug trade. One thing is for sure: I was confused!

But, as I said, everything had now changed. I had enough reason, in my mind, to do what I was doing, what with Vick's potential legal difficulties and my children hanging in the balance.

Now? Now it was on! What I did with Vick was for his sake. Everything else now had a different agenda—equally important to me—my only hope of getting my children back.

Walking a fine line became my rule of the day. I had no problem assisting in getting dealers off the street. However, I had a massive problem with the current method used towards users by the cops—arrest them all and let the courts and jail sort it out. I believed there was a better answer.

A not-uncommon conversation between Victor C and me:

"Who all was in the house?"

"I've told you who was dealing. I've told you who sold to the dealer. I've also told you I won't help you bust users."

Victor C didn't like it, but that was as far as I was willing to go. If somebody graduated to dealing, I always told him.

And it was the users who broke my heart the most. Methamphetamine has a wicked effect on the brain. It alters the way the brain functions. The hallucinatory and paranoid effects create shortcuts in the brain that are never meant to be there. But, the impact of those effects is destructive in the user's life.

What could I do? To say the least, as is evident from my life, I'm a doer and a fixer. The washing machine broke, I fixed it. The computer malfunctioned; I reprogrammed it. The piano's out of tune; I tuned it. I cannot help the urge- and if a person is broken, I'll put forth the effort to help.

But seriously, what could I do?

And you need to understand the intricacies of my situation. I lived in the gray area of the law. Some of my actions were illegal. The only reasons I would not be in trouble were, number one, I didn't do foolish things in public, and number two, I had the backing of the law enforcement community. The latter didn't make my actions any less illegal; it only kept me from picking up charges. The former was a risk I was sometimes willing to take.

I had become a full-time driver for drug dealers. Initially, it was only for Vick. After the aforementioned Tuesday, it became anyone who'd hired me. In the process, by association, I became involved in many things—stealing, fights, attacks, and gun-running, to name just a few. And all the while keeping my handler, Victor C, aware of my actions.

I kept my eye on the prize—getting my young friend out of the business. I didn't know how long the sheriff's department would drag its feet, but I would have to stay engaged at all costs. They had me in a position from which I could not easily extricate myself, and the price would be high if I tried. But, if it meant being the get-away driver from a shop-lifting spree, so be it. If I even had to participate, I would, but I would have to be smart about it.

When trouble was avoidable, I dodged it. Once, because I had a valid I.D., I was tasked with returning stolen merchandise to a store for a refund. It was not too expensive but enough to complete a drug transaction. They could not return it themselves. It was late, and they'd just stolen it. I met them in the parking lot, took the item to the return desk, and returned it with the following statement to the clerk,

"Look, I have to stand here for a minute and make this attempt, but know this was stolen. I am doing some freelance work with the police. So talk to me for a minute, shake your head in case someone's watching, and put it behind your counter."

It took her a minute to digest what I was saying, and then she played along. It was a good thing, for when I turned around, one of the girls with the dealer had followed me and was watching from nearby.

This close call convinced me several times to carry through with the task given. It would not be worth my life or health, and it was okay with Victor C, for he continued to encourage my efforts.

Then, a trip back from Atlanta one night set a new high mark of terror. I had gone up with one dealer to a high-rise hotel and waited for him to go upstairs and come back. He did come back with four people in tow—all carrying weapons. And remember, by this point, I was Unk to everybody.

"Hey, Unk! You don't mind giving these guys a lift down to Thomaston, do you?"

What was I supposed to say?

"Sure. Hop in!"

And I got an education. One in a way I don't ever want to repeat!

Driving for an hour-and-a-half with spun-out and high drug dealers doing weapons checks is not fun, not to mention the occasional wave of a pistol, and one pointed at me because they thought it was funny.

I did come up with helpful information. Though loosely tied together, this was without question an organization. This was not what I was used to. I knew plenty of dealers like Vick. They'd buy from different "weight" dealers depending on who had the best deal. No, these folks were tied in. They got their dope from a Mexican cartel. They not only traded in methamphetamine, but they also handled lots of weight in cocaine, heroin, and weapons. These were not your local gangbangers or garage dealers, and they were dangerous people.

I laughed at their jokes. I drove carefully. I made them my friends. I now had an intro to the top of the chain.

It was the middle of the night. Neither Victor C. nor Greg answered their phones. That made perfect sense. Most of my work was in the middle of the night. Most of theirs during the day, and it was one of their many excuses, but they sure kept me engaged. I left a message.

"Look, these are some nasty people, but this is a chance to make a real difference. They're running guns, cocaine, heroin, but they are terrible people, and they're organized. I'm not calling them the mafia, but they have a hierarchy,"

or something very close to that.

I was most assuredly afraid of these people. There was a lot to fear, but this would be precisely what I needed. This was a big-ticket item, would make more than just a dent in the drug trade, and would get a letter to the juvenile court correcting the lies others had told about me. Of course, it would not do anything about my young friend, but for the life of me, I did not understand what he was still doing on the streets.

I didn't hear back from either message. When I brought up the possibility of bringing them down in a phone conversation, Victor C. summarily dismissed it.

This event was something that would only add to my fears later.

The more I engaged with these people, the more information I could obtain, and I inserted myself at every opportunity. And it got pretty close to home. I had become one of them, and my father's house had become a stopping-off place. I needed something different, but I had nowhere else to go. I kept telling myself the cops would not be much longer, and I could not let these people in the house, so I did the next best thing. I moved into the large storage building behind the house and turned it into living quarters. Dad didn't like it, but it kept the traffic out of his house.

"Going in deeper" meant a lot of things. It meant engaging with dangerous people. It meant dealing with those lost in their addictions. It meant playing my role to a "T," and after several months, it began to take its toll. It meant getting my hands dirty. It meant getting my soul dirty.

At some point, staying involved and doing it safely without using becomes impossible. I don't care who you are, and I don't care what anybody says; you cannot get the kind of information I was securing without being one of them. I would never have gained their trust. So, I could only hide behind the "I only do dope by myself" excuse for a while.

After Tuesday's court, it was impossible. It was them 24/7 or stop, and my handler had me over a barrel with Vick. Quitting meant leaving him behind. My situation with my children left me with no other option. I had to find a way to overcome the impossible—a juvenile court's unfair decision. I had to become a real hero at whatever personal cost to me.

"In my mind."

Some of you who read the last paragraph sympathized with me and agreed. The rest of you? I know, that's about the craziest rationalization you've ever read. But it is where I was. I had left Christ's leading in my life.

The truth is I didn't know how to follow His leadership.

Following Christ is no halfway measure. It's an all-or-nothing proposition. When you're not all the way, you'll find yourself justifying all kinds of behavior—probably not as drastic as I did, but some of you need to look in the mirror.

I also know what some of you are thinking. "This is a perfect example of an addict finding an excuse to use!" You would not be wrong. I liked the high—I couldn't stand the aftereffects. The few times previously in my life I'd used meth, it didn't last too long. And I'll not tell a lie. I didn't just use when I had to. Like following Christ, drug use becomes an all-or-nothing compulsion. Regrettably and sadly, I used, but I longed for it to end. I understood the risks of meth use the longer it stayed in my system.

The sheriff's department seemed not to want to

keep their end of the agreement, and beyond doubt, they were using me and my information as long as they could drag it out.

It was transparent; law enforcement cared nothing for my safety. After months of daily reports and pleas for them to do something, all they gave me were excuses for not making the arrest that mattered, but they made plenty of other arrests of people connected to Vick. I guess they thought I was stupid and didn't notice. In reality, I had someone I cared more about than their opinions of me.

Their complete ambivalence towards me, personally, came not too long after that Tuesday. In all my drug use, I had never been a banger, slammer, or whatever you want to call an intravenous drug user. It wasn't what I considered an intelligent thing to do. So Victor C's response to my desperate call one day was telling.

"Victor, this has got to come to an end! Four months isn't long enough to figure things out? These are not nice people. I've told you. I can handle the threats and care for myself, but today takes the cake! Two of these guys thought it'd be funny to jam a needle in my arm, so they held my arm down and stuck the crap in."

"Really?" was his response.

"Really, Vick. I didn't feel a thing, but that's irrelevant. I've never slammed on my worst day. You all need to work this out! I'm over it."

"You didn't feel anything? Well, go home and rest. You'll be alright."

Wow! Missing a vein for you who have never crossed the intravenous line feels like someone set your arm on fire. I now also know from personal experience. Could I have fought the two guys off? Probably. Did I not out of some sick addict curiosity? Probably, but it doesn't take much of the burn to make you stay still. And I was honest. I didn't feel a thing. Fifteen prior years of cocaine use set my tolerance level pretty high for any amphetamine. The shot wasn't big enough. I now know from personal experience gained at my own hands.

Talk about "caught between two worlds!" And this was no blissful green C. S. Lewis, Chronicles of Narnia, "Wood Between the Worlds." This was a tentative, at best, grasp on the real world, isolated and alone, while diving into a pool leading to a world of destruction and chaos. I had no anchor in sanity. I'd left Christ behind. My Dad was the only other person who knew, and he disapproved. The cops could've cared less. I was on my own.

I'd chosen this world in which to reside. The cops promised two weeks, and I might have gotten out at any time, but the cost would have been high; however, no one made me stay. I was "in for a penny, in for a pound!"

I was a candidate if they gave awards for these types of performances. I had no real balance, but if anything were close, I would find it. The users needed help, and I was dead set on not letting the law be their answer. I'd already suffered through that option on my own. I wouldn't be a part of state-enforced rehab for any user. A dealer spun out like my young friend? Without question, it was his only hope.

I cared, and I cared deeply, but what could I do? So I tried the impossible—intervention from the inside. I know there are a lot of addicts reading this who just had to stop reading and dry their eyes after laughing at me so hard!

At best, I was in a precarious position—playing both sides of the fence.

If someone had stranded themselves, I'd pick them up. If they needed somewhere to sleep, I'd put them up in the spare room—no drug use allowed in the house. I babysat children. I helped pay missed bills.

I was enabling but also trying to meet people where they were. This whole thing had to end soon. If I were to have any currency with them, I figured when they were in need was an excellent time to get it. I wanted them to be able to hear me later. Completely useless? No. Many people I was acquainted with then are clean now and even follow my blog. Utterly stupid? Well, yeah, I was.

Trying to be kind but playing the role of one easily duped was a bad combination. I would lose thousands of dollars of tools. Before I finally gave up and hit the road walking, everything I owned had been stolen—down to my socks and my last pair of underwear.

I was open game, and by connection, so was Dad. By this point, it was chaos only the cops could end, and they were okay with what it cost me, so long as one of two possibilities was true. One, they were happy making many arrests because they looked good, or two, protecting someone more valuable than I was. Was there a dirty cop? I don't know, but I had room for suspicion.

I had been left hung out to dry. Things would only go from bad to worse!

April 20, 2018

The chest pains returned today. It's never a good thing. The jail released me on an O.R. bond and dropped me at the emergency room door. At least tonight, I'll rest easier in the hospital.

The past two days pushed my stress level to the max. So, instead of Spelding County releasing me, they put me in a cell block with 20 or so guys that I was in some way responsible for being locked up.

I don't know who knows what I've been doing for the sheriff's department, and their propensity to leave me unprotected is now without question.

After everything I've gone through with attempts on my life, I've just had to spend two days masquerading again while constantly wondering who would throw me off the top railing.

It's no wonder I'm in the hospital. Kudos to the E.R. docs. I was hardly in the E.R. before they had admitted me. I've got tests scheduled for Monday. Maybe I can calm down enough by then. At least I'm free.

15

Pre-heated

How long could I hang on? You'll get no argument from me. My grasp on reality was tentative, at best. Total immersion in a drug subculture is destructive enough to people who want to be there. Natural paranoia, exacerbated at times by drug-induced fear, was stretching me beyond this human's capacity to have anything close to sanity, and yet, I continued to function.

My daily reports continued to flow, including an almost daily request to end this. I continued to hold a job. I picked up my children nearly every weekend, during which time, staying away from the drug crowd was a necessity but becoming increasingly difficult.

The days and weeks passed in a blur of confusion, exhaustion, stress, and desperation. Even now, looking back, the order of events is unclear to me, and I lived through them.

Six months in, my young friend was still on the streets wreaking havoc. Six months in, and Special Operations was still making excuses. Six months in, and I should have walked away from it. It had become evident the cops were no better than the criminals. Everybody ran amok!

Four events stick out in my mind from that period. One would be the beginning of the end of my willingness to tell anything to the sheriff's department. One would scare the life out of me for Vick. And two would almost take my life.

****

I got a call. Some folks were coming in from South Carolina hoping to score some decent weight. They were looking for six ounces. Dealers, including Vick and a couple of others for whom I drove, had been called. The supply was a little dry, and the weight needed to be present when they arrived. It would be a free-for-all as to who could come up with the quantity, and all of them wanted to include me.

If I managed to stay in the middle of it, perhaps I would finally get what I wanted—Vick out and a bust worthy of "hero" status. After all, this was a decent amount of dope. It was interstate trafficking. It had the makings of what I desperately needed.

So, I stayed with it all day. I waited as the proverbial ping-pong ball bounced back and forth about who could provide the large amount of meth requested. Despite being surrounded by users and dealers, I stayed in touch with Special operations all day.

Waiting in the parking lot of the hotel where I was employed, I finally got the call. The dope was on the way.

I called Victor C.

"It's on the way. We're supposed to meet them in the North Gate parking lot. These are not good people. I'm more than a little afraid."

The equivocations began.

"David, I don't know if I can mobilize enough people to get up there."

"What do you mean? I've been telling you about this all day. Now, it's about to go down!"

"We can't do anything about it. You need to get yourself out of it."

Get myself out of it? I had been inserting myself into the middle of it all day! So what'd he mean, "Get yourself out of it?" If I extricated myself, I'd lose traction and credibility. I wasn't about to stay involved, but as my heart dropped, I realized I was about to take a severe hit in the ground gained through my efforts. Oh, you better believe I was angry.

Then something odd happened. I got another call. Something had spooked the two guys from South Carolina. They left right before the dope arrived and drove straight back to South Carolina empty-handed. It was odd. Despite our best efforts, they'd waited all day. They'd been patient. They weren't sitting around getting high and paranoid. Had they been warned away? That was the question bouncing around inside my head. I was never notified again when the S.C. guys returned until after they had come and gone. Red flags were flying!

Questions abounded, and disenfranchisement with the sheriff's department grew.

****

"Unk! I think I killed somebody!"

With that exclamation, my initial fears were realized. Wasn't this one of the reasons I had begun this in the first place? Intervene before he killed someone or got killed?

"What happened?"

He proceeded to tell me. A black man had tried to molest a child. He had chased the man down in a van, run him over, jumped out, and beat the man with a tire iron. The bad thing was? He was in my van.

"Vick, you don't come back from killing somebody. Dude! What were you thinking?"

"I wasn't thinking. I lost it!"

I knew exactly what he was talking about. Several months prior, I'd seen it all in my driveway when a chemical flood washed away inhibitions and good sense. He was 30 minutes away in Barnesville.

"Bring me my van back. Let me see what I can find out."

I called my handler.

"Is this not enough?" I almost shouted at him.

"There's nothing reported. But, I'll check into it," was his response.

A few hours later, I discovered an ambulance had picked up the man. He was alive and eventually recovered. However, when I approached my handler about the subject a couple of weeks later, he was dismissive.

"No report was ever filed. No victim, no crime."

It had been swept under the rug, but why? Whatever kept me feeding them information? I was done with them. My effort to help my young friend—as screwed up as my attempt might have been—was fruitless.

****

It was midnight, late in November, and I was in bed. I had begun backing out of driving opportunities. It was pointless, as far as Vick was concerned. The only thing keeping me engaged was Greg—the Special Operations member seconded to the DEA. I hoped I could do something with the DEA through Greg to gain traction with the juvenile court. I was taking a few days off. My body couldn't hold up at the pace I had been on.

My phone awakened me. It was someone I'd driven for on one previous occasion.

"Hey, Unk! Vick just left me stranded, and I need a ride home."

Mustang had acquired a vehicle, and despite lacking a driver's license, he was currently handling his own transportation. Of course, he'd done that before, but at best, it never lasted more than a few days or weeks.

I shook the sleep out of my eyes and turned onto the highway before I realized I'd left my glasses on my nightstand, a mistake proving catastrophic.

Squinting through the foggy night air, I went to run the person home. All I wanted was to go and come back. My bed had been comfortable. I picked her up and made the long drive out into the country to take her home.

"Come on in, Unk. Let me get you paid."

I acquiesced. The house and yard were full of people. The drugs were flowing. Several people pulled up. One was my young friend. One was one of the two who had attempted to stick a needle in my arm two months before.

He made the threat again with what I couldn't tell was real menace or joking. I didn't want anything, but his face wasn't visible in the dim light. I told him I'd do it myself. With a slight miss, I pulled the still-full needle out, tossed it to the floor, and made to leave. At this point, he commented something about the cops related to me. I was skittish enough. I already suspected I had been discovered. I didn't know this guy well, and I was afraid.

I made my excuses and bolted for the door. I got in my van and sped out of the long drive, hitting the road and going too fast.

I made it to the first curve in the road, going about 55 mph. Lacking my glasses on a dark, foggy night, I saw the turn too late. So, the van flipped, and I ended up upside-down, in a ditch, knocked out by the far side when I collided with it through the windshield of my van.

I don't remember much after seeing the ditch rushing toward my face. Vick was the one who dragged me from the van as flames eagerly licked at the gas tank. I know the first responders wanted to life-flight me to a trauma unit in Atlanta. It was quicker for the ambulance to travel at breakneck speed to deliver me to a level one trauma center, and the paramedics thought I'd broken my neck.

I awakened in the hospital hours later. Dad, very concerned, had arrived and was near my side. An E.R. doctor entered my room and began to excoriate and harangue me.

"We've wasted our time on you tonight. You have no real serious injuries. You have no broken bones, and you're a drug addict. You're a waste of our time!"

In essence, that's what he said in about a ten-minute speech, and he used those words over and again! Part of me understands. I had a swollen left arm from the slight miss, but I doubt I had any significant quantity of drugs in my system. With a needle mark on my arm, he had determined my worth!

I was hot. Roiling in my mind was I'd worked for months against the very thing he was accusing me of, but I couldn't blame the doctor. He didn't know. He did know I'd just survived a serious accident. I didn't deserve the treatment he gave me, but I understood, which made me angrier.

"No significant injury? Then I'm leaving!" I blew back at him.

"Leave the neck brace! You can't have it," he said, storming out of the room.

The door was not shut before a nurse hurried in.

"Sir! You cannot leave. He misspoke. You don't have any broken bones, but you have significant injuries. They may very well result in paralysis or other complications. You need to stay. He's wrong. Please stay."

There was that word "significant," and I was significantly angered, for sure. I tossed her the neck brace.

"I'm leaving."

The nurse brought me a wheelchair and rolled me out. I may have been wrong, but I wouldn't be talked to that way.

Chaos was at full rein in my life. It was my fault, and consolation was not to be had.

April 21

Well, doesn't that just fit?! The hospital administrator came around this morning. He had discovered I had no insurance.

"Mr. Riordan, your vitals leveled out overnight. I think you should go home and come back Monday for the tests we have scheduled." And just like that, I was escorted from the hospital! I had become quite used to it, only this time, there had been no drugs in my system for some time. It was all about the insurance.

I couldn't call Dad. His last words to me a couple of weeks ago had been, "Don't ever step foot on my property again." Of course, in the intervening time, I had borrowed his R.V. That didn't go over so well, as it turns out, and those people were still in his house. Maybe one day, he'd understand.

I called Dan. He will let me spend the night in his house and take me to church tomorrow morning. I only have a few options left. At least nobody knows I'm still in town. I have to get out of town. I'm out of options.

16

Into the Oven

With the wreck, the proverbial camel's back was broken. I sent a message to Victor C. withdrawing any future help.

I turned around and sent one to Greg, reaffirming my willingness to work with him. We talked, and he brought up paying me again. He repeated his desire to expunge my record, at least. I would not turn that down. Erasing my criminal history would have the same impact as a letter to the courts.

Recovering from my injuries, I began the new year reinvigorating my efforts. Mustang drifted from my concerns. The DEA had not made any concessions for my young friend. I wouldn't involve him in anything in the future.

I had made plenty of contacts. I needed to cultivate those relationships, which would take some effort. But, by the second week of January, I had what I needed.

I had come across a certain ne'er-do-well whose favorite movie character was the Joker and who went by the moniker of "WhySoSerious." Seriously. Like so many before him, he required transportation, and like others before him, he wasn't a worthy target, but he knew those worth going after by the DEA. So, I needed to use him to get to those.

I gave him a ride to Stone Mountain, the community, not the mountain itself. He made a purchase. I passed the information off to Greg, as I always had for anybody not in Spelding County. Greg took the data with no commitment to me, and a couple of days later, my new contact in Stone Mountain was arrested with pounds of heroin and methamphetamine, earning trafficking charges. The information proved itself out, and we removed significant quantities of drugs from the Marketplace!

I took another trip into Henry County, but I was a passenger this time, not the driver, and it was not fruitful. We arrived at a house, and my new friend owed them a lot of money. Threats flew. I exited the house as they were attempting to cut off his finger. By the night's end, he talked his way out of this situation, but these were not pleasant people, and I didn't make the mistake of being a passenger again.

I left and caught a ride with a Henry County sheriff's deputy, and I hate to say it, but it was the brightest law enforcement spot during this whole dark time of my life. I wasn't dressed appropriately; he might have saved my life from the cold.

My new friend returned the following day with ten fingers still intact, apologizing profusely. He also explained this was the same group I had run into before that was running drugs directly from and guns to Mexico. One would be in town, not too far from where I lived. He wanted a sample from a lower-level dealer to set up a purchase for the day after the next.

I told him I'd think about it.

I called Greg.

"Can you set it up for a quarter pound Friday afternoon?"

"I can set it up for as much as you'd like."

"Let's keep it at ¼ pound, and don't worry about the money; they'll never make it to you. Have the drop set up for your house."

"Greg, I don't like it. It puts my dad's house in jeopardy."

"They'll never get that far. They won't even cross the Spelding County line before we have them."

Books need a soundtrack. If one were playing right now, eerie-sounding impending doom music would build toward a crescendo.

I returned to my storage building/tiny home to talk to Arthur, "Why So Serious." Covering for my short absence, I said,

"I will have to borrow the money from Dad, but I can have it all together by Friday. This will set me up nicely."

Arthur wanted me to drive him ½ mile to pick up his sample for immediate use. That ride would take place several hours after the sun was down, and the lack of sun would not be the only darkness in the night.

"Hey, you're broke. Right?"

Nodding my head, "I've got nothing."

"These guys will take a trade. Have you got anything worth a few bucks? I'll get us something."

"I thought this was supposed to be a sample. Samples are free."

He then launched into a contrived answer as to why he needed currency of some sort. I understood. He owed them money. He wasn't going to get anything for free. I was so used to fiction that I hardly batted an eyelash. However, I could only think everything would soon be over. I would extricate myself from this mess on Friday, less than 48 hours away. I didn't care what it took. I'd have given up about anything by this point.

"I've got a T.V. and an old cell phone. Will that work?"

Throwing the stuff in the back of the truck, we took the short ride. And he started with the stupid stuff.

"You gotta wait outside. This guy's kinda sketchy. You know how they get."

I didn't care. I had my life set on coast. It was 36 hours and counting. I was so done with it! So I acquiesced and waited outside, and waited, and waited, and waited.

It was not unusual in the meth world to wait. It was probably the second most significant reason I never got hung up on methamphetamine. You are always waiting on a dealer, and they never do what they say they will do. Besides, I wasn't waiting for Arthur to come out. I was waiting on Friday. He could take as long as he wanted to, and my waiting might not be something the real me would do, but it was something this me would, so I was okay!

Two hours later, Arthur came out agitated.

"They kept your stuff and wouldn't give me the dope!"

I may have developed a persona of an easy pushover, but it was never safe to be considered one to be taken advantage of. Besides, I could talk myself out of almost anything and had to think about what was expected of a man. Plus, this dealer had connections to the upcoming Friday transaction. I couldn't let this pass and maintain the deal on Friday. Regardless of what the dealer now had, I had to make a showing at least.

If I had seen the truth, I would never have walked through the door. I am not often blind-sided. This night was an exception.

A guy answered the door, and I spoke,

"Hey, let me come in and talk to y'all for a minute."

He was too nice. That should have been my first sign. I missed it. He shut the door behind me and led me through the back of the house. Turning left, he reached the kitchen and reached his hand out. I was suddenly no longer fooled, for he had a hammer in his hand swinging it at my head!

Everything happened so fast, but my memory is in slow motion. I spent my life in construction, and I know hammers. I snatched the hammer from his hand before it connected with my head. I slung it at him, hitting him in the head. That's when I saw the second person swinging at me, and I took him down with one hit. Then, not realizing the totality of the danger I was in, I grabbed the first guy halfway to the floor and lost the fight. After that, I only remember a boot driving my head back with my body behind it, carrying the first man backward.

As I lost consciousness from multiple people kicking me from head to toe, my last thought was, "I was set up!"

What happened next came to me through eyewitness accounts several weeks later. I don't remember anything.

They continued to batter my body and head with kicks. Five began the beatdown, but I had been able to weaken the force down to three. I was an employed construction worker. They were spun-out drug addicts.

The grandfather of the young man who also lived there saved my life. The older man yelled, "I called the cops, and they're on the way!"

They cleared the house. Two helping two, and my "friend," Arthur, also running away. He had been a part of it, kicking and hitting from behind. But, of course, I didn't know this because I was unconscious. I had been done in by four men and a woman. I had taken two down with me. Not bad for an older man, but it didn't matter. It was not a win for me unless you consider staying alive a win.

Concussed, a bloody mess, and blue jeans ripped into shreds from waist to ankles, somehow I managed to climb to my feet, walk out to my truck, and drive away before the cops arrived. I don't have a clue how. I have no memory.

What I did makes no sense, but it is what I did. I drove to my friend Billy's house several miles into the country and banged on his door. Nobody answered, and I dropped my one-of-a-kind in Griffin, Georgia, Alaska cap on the porch. I got back in the truck and drove home.

And here, my memory returned for a moment before I lapsed into the welcome darkness of oblivion. I remember changing pants. I must not go to the hospital in ripped jeans! That would be unpalatable.

The next moment is etched clearly into my memory because it's so surreal I still chuckle about it today despite my circumstances at the time.

Remember who my father is: well-respected, outstanding community leader, and upright lay leader of the church, and he ruled his home with an iron fist while I was growing up. I revere the man! Any respect not shown to him during this time of my life was by necessity. I calculated every move I made. I had to. My life depended on it.

After my brain-fogged exercise of changing pants and still bleeding heavily, I barged into his bedroom and flipped on the light. You don't do that to my dad, but I was certainly not in my right mind. Spitting out a tooth, I looked at Dad and said,

"I think I need to go to the hospital."

Wow! What an understatement, and I blacked out again!

Several hours later, I awakened in the emergency room, bandaged, and my other injuries attended to. I had broken bones, injuries to my left arm and leg, nose, and back, a concussion and a crushed left hand, and 24 broken teeth out of the 28 I had left, but I was alive.

And the end of this chapter in my life was within spitting distance. So, all I had to do was be there Friday.

Once again, I signed myself out of the hospital. I lied to the sheriff's deputy who interviewed me at the hospital and said I had no idea who did this. In my mind, nothing was worth ruining Friday!

The following morning, though I was no longer connected to Spelding County, I called Victor C.

"Look, I've got something going on with Greg. You should already know about it. You should know I lied to the deputy at the hospital. It should be easy enough for them to investigate because one of the jerks lives in the house where it happened, but I cannot officially say anything."

"I'll make sure they handle it right," he said.

Two hours later, I knew all five names, though I didn't learn of Athur's involvement until later, and with that future revelation, I now know how close I was to death.

Months later, not so surprisingly, Spelding County didn't have a single suspect, and things that made me question everyone's allegiances continued to pour in!

Then, it was a matter of calling Greg. I could barely stand, but it was so on! The end was in sight!!

****

Banged up and bruised, I made the call early to Greg. I had already called Mr. "Why So Serious" Arthur. Everything was in motion. The delivery was set for noon or one o'clock.

"I've already told you. These folks scare me. I don't like that you've got them aiming at Dad's house."

"David, you've just got to trust us. We'll pick them up coming through Tara. They'll never make it into Spelding County."

"I hear you, but you know how bad I'm hurt right now. I can't run, and I have no money. I know I'm just nervous, But I have reason to be!"

"Don't worry about it. We'll cover our end. Now, any information you can get from your contact will help. When they'll be coming through—Which car they'll be in for sure."

"It's not like I can come right out and ask them. That's the kinda stuff that'll get me killed."

"Do your best and stay in touch."

Then it became a game. Engage with Arthur often and long enough, and just let him speak. That was my plan, and it worked. Arthur loved to talk, and I listened. Soon, I had more information than I cared to have.

"They'll be in a small white 4-door sedan—a Toyota Corolla. But listen, the guy driving is dangerous. I've never met him, but I know him by reputation. His nickname is the Chinaman. He recently got out of prison for manslaughter a few months ago. Greg, I'm more than a little concerned. This guy's not going to pull over for you. As soon as he sees blue lights, he's running. Make no mistake about it! Whatever method you have to box him in is what y'all better do. They'll not get here til at least two. They'll be coming through Jonesboro thirty minutes before that or later. They will not be early. They never are."

Greg was dismissive of my warning again. I talked to him at least 5 or 6 times after that and warned him every time. My nerves were as ragged as my trust in the cops, but it was almost over! I texted him the warning. I did about everything but shouted from the rooftops.

"David, you need to call them and find out where they are! We haven't spotted them, and plenty of cars are out looking."

I shook my head to myself. These folks had no idea how hard it was for me to get any information. Dealers are already massively paranoid, even if they didn't use their own supply, and about every meth dealer uses. I've never met one who didn't.

I pondered. I worried. I concocted reasons to call and couldn't come up with one, but I didn't have to because my phone rang, and looking down, I saw Arthur's name on the screen.

"Hey, Unk. We got held up in Lovejoy. This crazy girl wanted to stop at Walmart. I think she's in there trying to lift stuff."

"You've gotta be kidding me! You've got what I wanted. Yes?"

"Of course."

"Why in the hell would you even stop? Dude, that's just about stupid. Glad you don't already have my money." Keeping the pressure on him eased the pressure on me, and sounding aggravated and anxious covered my genuine fear.

"We'll be on our way shortly."

"Well, hurry."

I phoned Greg.

"They're in Lovejoy at the Walmart."

"I don't know how they got past us. I'm not that far away. I can be there in about five minutes. Call them and see if you can slow them down."

What was I, some kind of magician?

"You've got time. They've got a couple of people in the store. You'll be alright. Just hurry."

This was going great. Not! I had no nerves left. I was in pain and scared out of my mind, and the people I depended on had let them slip through!

Greg called. He couldn't find them.

Arthur called. They were getting a burger.

Greg called. He still couldn't find them.

Arthur called, "Man, you wouldn't believe it. I almost got in a car with the Chief of Police up here. It was crazy. Don't know what I was thinking, but we're headed that way."

Greg called, "I found them. You won't believe what that fool did. He almost got in the car with me."

I know. It sounds like something from a "comedy of errors" movie. The only problem was that no one seemed too concerned with my life. So, I wasn't too interested in laughing.

They were 15 miles away. 20 minutes. It was this close to success or this close to doom.

Closing my eyes didn't help.

Twenty minutes is a long time. I paced in the street. I went inside and got a Diet Coke and couldn't drink it. You know I had to be stressed! My heart was about to pound out of my chest. I looked at my phone, paced some more, walked outside, and went back in.

Rinse and repeat!

Thirty minutes went by. Things must be okay. If I'd known what had happened, I'd have had a heart attack on the spot and not have lived to tell the story. But, if this ordeal had yet to be botched enough, law enforcement wanted to ensure they did it right!

They ignored every one of my warnings. Instead, they did everything they said they would NOT do. Tailing the dealer from Lovejoy, they followed right on over the Spelding County line and continued for 7.7 miles until the car turned right onto my street—less than two-tenths of a mile from where I was pacing in the middle of it. They had waited until he turned onto my dead-end road before hitting the lights, and they tried to stop him with one car.

There's no suspense here. You gotta know what the "Chinaman" did. He ran!

He did a 180, whipping into the veterinary clinic's parking lot at the corner and spinning his wheels onto the congested US 19/41. It was the beginning of rush hour, and the road was packed. The "Chinaman" lost the pursuit for about thirty seconds when he dipped around some traffic running through the grassy median, at which point, his passengers dumped the dope and a bunch of hypodermic needles. Once back on the road, he floored it. He didn't make it far; driving 80 miles an hour, he ran headlong into an old oak tree.

Of course, I was oblivious, still pacing, trying not to chew the ends of my fingers off with the nails. I had missed the twenty seconds of excitement at the end of my street. I think I'm glad I did! Then, an hour later, Greg called. I was relieved—for a second.

"David, how much meth were they supposed to have?"

"I don't know. They started with a pound, is what they said. You know I was only supposed to get a ¼ of that. They very well could have gotten rid of the other before they got here."

"They don't have anything on them. We're going to have to check the road. They got away from the pursuit for a few seconds. We got the driver. You're right. He's a bad one."

I shook my head in silence!

It was over, at least for me. I knew it from the bottom of my heart. And it was all for nothing. I tried several more times over the next few months, but my heart wasn't in it, and my credibility was trashed.

What had I been doing? Crushing defeatism plagued my every thought. Nothing made sense. My entire existence was futile. Everything I owned had been stolen except the clothes on my back. I had not a single tool left, and my whole family hated me!

Making matters worse, my young friend was now in jail. They hadn't caught him with drugs but would drag him as long as possible. So, he was out of my hands.

Adding to my misery, in my attempts to help others, my dad had misread my intentions and hired one of the addicts I knew to work as a housekeeper for him. Trying to defraud him, she stirred his anger against me, figuring she could take advantage of him if she got rid of me. My actions had not helped his opinion of me.

Talk about a mess? And I have only scratched the surface. As the reality of my failures became all-pervasive, depression, and self-hate became my constant companions. However, as things coalesced in my mind and pieces fell into place, anxiety replaced depression, and disgust would soon morph into abject fear.

Word began to filter back to me that a Special Operations Deputy had told someone I was an informant. It was not an unusual accusation in the meth world for everybody else. The funny thing is, in all the time I had worked with the cops, I had only been accused once, and the accusation lasted about five minutes. Everybody in the meth subculture, including my young friend, was accused of being an informer. Here, I was definitively working for law enforcement, and they never figured it out.

In fear, my mind began to work overtime. Too many things didn't add up, like law enforcement's inability to make a clean bust of my young friend. I thought I had it figured out, but did I? Certain people could get away with things, and others couldn't. Then I discovered Arthur had been in on the attempt on my life, and even after the high-speed chase with definitive input from me, he walked free of any charges.

Then, the threats began. Keeping only very loose ties with dealers, I began extricating myself from the lifestyle. Yet, suddenly, I felt my life was in more danger than ever. Things were getting rather inhospitable in my hometown. I had to leave.

I'd had enough. It was April 10. I had been warned to get out of town. I heeded the warning. I loaded up what little I had in Dad's R.V., wrote him a letter, and left it with one of the new household residents in my dad's home. Of course, Dad would not be happy, but hopefully, the letter would explain enough.

As I pulled out of the driveway, a drug deal was going down in a car in my dad's driveway. I had no one to call. There was no one I trusted. Despite my efforts, I couldn't even keep the drugs off my dad's property. I was a complete failure.

I pulled out onto the highway. A. sheriff's deputy was sitting at the end of my street. I put gas in the R.V., which was the end of my money. I'd have to go as far as possible and beg for more gas. That would have to be my plan.

Then came the blue lights in my rearview mirror. Wondering what I'd done wrong, I rolled the window down. The officer grilled me about where I was going and if I was leaving right then. Whatever concerns I had with imagination washed away. All the cop was concerned about was whether I was leaving and how fast I would be gone. Things added up, and I didn't like the sum. I left immediately.

One thing I felt for sure. I could not trust law enforcement in my town or anywhere close. So, I drove as fast as I could, heading northeast. I was leaving, and maybe for a long while. I had to see my two youngest children one more time. I was losing them, as I had lost everything else.

I began to feel better the further away I got, and my mind began to work. I needed to say something to somebody. I couldn't allow myself to get hemmed in, but my situation required investigation. And I was grasping at straws, but I might sit down with the sheriff of Moore County when I arrived. With bad blood between us, because he was married to my first ex-wife, I hoped somewhere deep inside, he could find the capacity to examine it or call the right person to begin an investigation.

On my way to Welsington, Georgia, the county seat of Moore County, I did find a willing ear in a retired State Trooper who now worked for the county next door to Moore. I had already run out of gas, and he helped me out. Listening to my story, he concurred that Moore County Sheriff Mick Marr would be a good starting place. I felt even better about the option.

Both of us could not have been more wrong. I would end up illegally detained for six days in Moore County Jail before being transported to Spelding County, where I would be thrown in a housing unit with many people I was responsible for having been locked up.

Fear, anxiety, and stress pushed every fiber of my being into a constant fight-or-flight mode. It's a simple fact. Our bodies were not made to take the totality of what I'd been through and my current situation. Despite my ability to make it through the past year, my body was no different from anyone else's. It broke.

I collapsed with chest pains. Rather than go through the expense of being guarded at the hospital, the Jailer released me on my own recognizance. I was unceremoniously dumped at the emergency room door by a deputy. After being admitted by the E.R., I was unceremoniously discharged the next day because I had no insurance.

With nowhere else to turn, I called my brother Dan, Vick's dad. Dan took me home with him. His wife was out of town. We spent the evening together, and on Sunday morning, he took me to church with him.

Something deep within me began to stir while being transported to Spelding County. The transport deputy was a Christian and ministered to me on a deeply spiritual level, and the music he played was unforgettable. The deputy had ignited a glimmer of a spark in my heart, fanning into a burgeoning flame of hope during Sunday School.

Oh, in no uncertain terms, I still had to leave town. There was no doubt. The threats from criminals were genuine. My lack of trust in law enforcement was all too plausibly reasoned. Even my last conversation with Greg had taught me no hope was coming from them. When I informed him someone had taken a shot at me, he discounted my story. When I mentioned the possibility of a dirty cop, he was in complete denial.

Yeah, I had to leave town!

That encouraging flame of hope began to warm me between Saturday night, April 21, and the following Sunday morning. Would God ever hear me again? After all, there might be a possibility, but only two options remained. My life was a wreck, a complete disaster. Outside my brother, not a single soul saw any value in me. I had been misused and abused, at the minimum, by law enforcement. The #100 crowd had trashed me—the criminal drug addicts who love to talk about honor but don't display it. My family had disowned me, and I had even lost my dog. (I know. I know. It sounds like the heart of a country song).

Two choices remained, and I wasn't the one who could make one of them. I was perfectly okay with dying. I didn't have anything to live for, anyway. If only God would hear me. That ball was entirely in His court.

THE BAKER'S STORY
MY SAGA

BOOK 2

THANK GOD, HE'S GOD
AND I'M NOT

OR

WHAT HE DID

OR

PRELUDE
TO A NEW KIND OF LIFE

Introduction

I could not in good conscience publish the prequel to my Prelude to a New Kind of Life without telling why it mattered. The substance and evidence of the life I now live are buried not in the life before but rather in how far God was willing to go to rescue such a wayward soul, for without Him, my life had no meaning. It is my life, but it is His story of redemption. It was my disaster, His new construction. It was my despair, His hope.

So, what follows is what followed, and it is what gives my life purpose. There were many vertical conversations along the way, and the very first was, for some reason, left out. Despondent and without real hope, I prayed, "Take me or take me. I cannot go on like this." It was the beginning of my surrender as I stepped out of my home county and into a new life.

When the second edition of the Prelude came out, it had a new thing. My oldest brother, the giver of the $15.00 you will soon read about, called me as I was polishing it up. "Dave, I hear music when I read your story." My thoughts were that it was just Dan. He lives and breathes music. "I'm going to write what I hear," he said, and he did. He would read a bit and translate the story into sound. Along with contributions from my nephew, the Baker Prelude Soundtrack was born.

What Dan and Timothy produced was beyond my imagination, but to this day, the strains take me back to my journey. I hear "Perplexity and Peace" and remember the Greyhound bus station and growing contentment. When I listen to "Walk of Faith," I often find myself inadvertently reaching to wipe the mud from my face. When "Helper" begins, and the eerie minor solo crosses paths with my ears, I hear His voice again for the first time.

Profound!

The Soundtrack can be found in the content section on theBakerandtheBread.com, and the music notes are delineated throughout the rest of this story. You will find the music takes you there, as it does me, but I also hope it transports you closer to my Savior, the Baker, my Lord Jesus Christ.

In Christ Alone
David Riordan
September 22, 2023

Track 1: Helper

April 22, 2018

I don't know that I will ever forget the desperation that washed over me as I stood on the edge of US 19/41, gazing north.

Almost without hope, I put one foot into Malier Road. In my mind, as I remember that step, I can hear that bass note sounding at the beginning of this song with the melancholy vocal coming in.

Desperation and Darkness.

The light at the end of the tunnel was not yet in my vision. But it was apparent to me and everyone around me that I could not do this on my own!

"So you should look for the LORD before it is too late. You should call to Him now, while He is near."

Isaiah 55:6 (ERV)

Foreword

In my many years of ministering to the down and out, I have heard a lot of people's stories. When this scruffy-looking fellow from our shelter approached me about attending our church services, I heard him out. He told me, with his country twang on fast forward, of his commitment to being obedient to God's leading. Even though I had heard similar stories many times before, when he began telling me his story, I was mesmerized. Whether it was his southern charm, his sincere heart, or the Spirit working through him, I was interested in what he had to say.

I told him the time our services began, and he actually showed up. He continued to show up faithfully. Soon, he started telling me of his desire to worship God through music. I informed him that he could have access to the piano. This enabled me to talk with David more often. Slowly, his story unfolded, and I couldn't help but feel compassion for him.

Eventually, he told me he was writing his story, and I asked him if I could read it. He agreed and gave me the first chapter, and I was hooked. He continued giving me more chapters. It was an incredible story that explained what brought about the faithfulness and obedience I had been seeing lived out in David's life. I realized that his tears, fears, and struggles about which we had talked only scratched the surface of what he had gone through.

With eloquence and wit, David has laid out his heart-wrenching story. I think it is a journey to which a vast majority of people can relate. Discovering the road he has traveled and his perseverance through trials will encourage anyone who has been there.

Read a few pages, and you will, without question, be eager to read one more page.

Thomas S. Babbitt, Major
The Salvation Army Cambridge, MA

Track 2: Escape

I had to leave. There was no doubt. However, running away is not synonymous with escaping. Ask the former resident of the frying pan.

It is not only necessary to know what or where you are leaving but the direction you must go to escape, as well.

I didn't have a clue as to where, but I did know to Whom I should run.

Partially written in Dorian mode, the hearer has difficulty determining in what key this piece is written.

However, as in my story, if you pay close attention with the uncertainty, and the unsettling need to go, you will also find the journey of discovery and victories along the way. Perhaps you will hear the rain
and the proverbial mountains I had to climb.

Surely, you will detect the relief of an answer received.

"I run for dear life to God, and I'll never live to regret it. Do what You do so well: get me out of this mess and up on my feet!"

Psalm 71:1, 2 (MSG)

17

Baked

"Drop me off at the RaceTrac," I said with all the confidence I did not feel. I did not have a choice. Behind me lay sorrow, pain, addiction, destruction, and death. Ahead of me—not a clue. It's funny how several people have lauded me recently for my step of faith at the time. In reality, I had no choice, no real choice, at any rate. "Surely, I can find a ride out of this place here" (one of the busiest gas stations in my hometown of Griffin, Georgia). I was wrong. As I gazed to the north, my intended egress, I saw nothing but heavy, overcast, black clouds in mid-afternoon, belying even the existence of the sun and seeking to erase any glimmer of hope that might exist deep inside me. But as I said, I had no real choice. No choice, I have discovered, is a great motivator in my life.

Into the gloom, I walked, and it started to rain-not much rain, just a constant drizzle—enough to be uncomfortable—certainly not enough to make me turn around. If I had only known, so I walked and walked. Two things were swirling in my head. One—one of my favorite songs is Keith Green's "O Lord You're Beautiful." And Two—My spoken refusal to God to curse Him because of my misery and die.

Not that I claimed to be Job in any shape, form, or fashion. I had had some misery and loss in my life.

After all, I was leaving my hometown, never to return, with the work boots on my feet, jeans, shirt, and leather jacket on my back—and the fifteen dollars my brother had just given me. "Now, Dave, I am not giving this to you to encourage you to leave. I think you should stay and face your problems," he said.

Of course, he had not had three recent attempts on his life.

Now, I don't get queasy at the sight of my blood. However, thirty years of construction experience have taught me that "if I don't see a little of my blood every day, I ain't workin'!" One of my oft-repeated, if not world-famous, mantras. That having been said, I did not want my life's blood flowing out through a small round hole.

I had to leave, and it made me miserable. Leaving underscored all the things and people I had lost to this point in my life and highlighted that it was my fault. I didn't dodge my own bullets or duck my own knife, but I had made choices. At the time, I felt not wrong choices but choices with consequences—one of those nasty things about life. Choices = consequences. I had made choices in the previous year with admirable intentions. However, we all know what paves the road to Hell.

I am not a stupid man—despite what some may think—I understood the potential outcome of those decisions. I was not in the least caught off guard. Every gambler knows he may lose it all. Every rock climber recognizes he may fall. Every builder understands the risk when he uses seconds for materials. The consequences could be catastrophic. I have done all three. Like most risk-takers, I view myself as a winner—denial being a great strength? Well, at least it shields us from pessimism.

I have also faced catastrophic consequences and still managed to survive. Survival = winning?

I admit it. I don't always think the way everyone else does. I view things a little differently –

no, scratch that

– a lot differently. I will give you a spoiler. I am wrong sometimes –

no, scratch that

– often.

I needed to have a conversation with my Father, one of those conversations you have as you are beginning to mature in life. The kind where you own up to something. "Dad, I wrecked the car." — "Dad, I need you to bond me out of jail." — "Dad, I don't have a bond this time. I need you to take care of some things for me." The kind of conversation where you admit you're wrong because you don't have any other reasonable choice, and you realize it—the kind where no one else is to blame.

"Father, I am in a bind."

I spiritually heard His response, "Boy, that don't take a rocket scientist to figure out."

"Yeah, I know. It is all my fault. You set me up with a task, and I accepted willingly—even excitedly."

"I knew you would—after all, I'm kinda in the position where I know everything, but Dave, why didn't you stick to the script?"

"Well, Father, I was excited and left the room before I read the script. I went out on my own. I was so intrigued by the job offer."

"Look, Dave, I know you. I knew you needed a script. I even wrote it for you, and others said their lines whether they realized it or not, but you ignored it. Instead, you went with your wisdom—with your script."

"Father, I was wrong."

"Well, you're in luck. I'm God, and you're not. I have this amazing ability to turn even the worst catastrophes into awesome, Me-glorifying things, so I want you to continue going until I tell you to stop."

"How will I know?"

"You'll know."

"Okay. Got a deal for you. I am selfish and self-centered. I don't even have an idea what I need."

"That's quite apparent, but I'm willing to work with you, anyway. So, what's your deal?"

"I won't ask anybody except you for anything. If you want me to have it, you will have to give it to me. If you don't want me to have it, don't give it to me."

"Deal. Let me make sure we're clear. I give you what I want, and you will thankfully receive it? I will withhold anything I think is wrong for you, and you'll be thankful for what I don't give you as well?"

"Yes, Father."

"It's about time. Now, keep walking, Dave."

"Yes, sir."

I walked and walked. Not a soul even seemed to notice my upturned thumb.

One thing I learned early in life was how to hike a challenging trail. My parents always planned two weeks of vacation every summer with the family. The first week was the action week in the, usually North Carolina Appalachian Mountains. The second week, we rested at Myrtle Beach, South Carolina. Rest was a relative term because the week of rest might include the following:

· A 6 a.m. jog down the beach to a fishing pier.

· A late-night jaunt to an inlet to gig for flounder or crabs.

· Riding "Rover" (a durable rubber raft) on the surf to see who might stay in it.

However, the hiking and backpacking trails in the North Carolina Appalachians taught the powerful lessons of durability and endurance. If you wanted to return to "civilization"—otherwise known as the campground—you had to put one foot in front of the other because no other options existed. Even if cell phones had been a thing then, no cell reception would have been available in some places we went so that you could forget "phone-a-friend" for a quick rescue. So, one chose between going nowhere or putting one foot in front of the other—no matter how tired you might be.

So, I walked. The sky cleared. That was cool. A car made a U-turn and pulled over in front of me. That was cooler. A young black man rolled down the window and asked me,

"Where are you headed?" That was the coolest. "As far north as you are," I replied. "Oh, well, you can hop in, but I am only headed to Walmart."

Even though I saw the Walmart sign in the distance, I hopped in. I was already tired, and any ride was better than no ride. I told him I appreciated the ride and was on a journey of faith and a Christian.

He glowed, “I’m kind of new to this life. I have just become a Christian and need to learn more about walking by faith.”

I felt the overwhelming sense God was at work in his life, and God had timed my walk with this young man’s U-turn. I felt the humbling realization that I was inadequate. I was not only financially bankrupt but spiritually bankrupt as well, or so I thought. Out of my mouth began to pour some well-placed words of wisdom impacting him profoundly. I discovered something in the 10 minutes I spent with this young man, talking and praying with him in the Walmart parking lot. I may have been spiritually bankrupt, but I had the keys to my heavenly Father’s spiritual bank. All I had to do was open the vault and let the wealth pour through me. After all, the spiritual wealth isn’t mine—it is God’s, and I can access it anytime He calls on me. My spirits rose. I felt encouraged. God wasn’t done with me yet. I walked out of the Walmart parking lot in Lovejoy, crossed the highway, stuck out my thumb—and it began to rain.

I walked a few more miles. Then, arriving in southern Jonesboro, as the rain began to fall in earnest, I glanced across the street and saw a church about to start services as people turned into the parking lot. Unusual, I thought, since most churches had shifted away from having Sunday night services.

It occurred to me that a dry place for an hour or so sounded good, and after my earlier experience, I felt like church would be good right about now. Even though I had been raised Southern Baptist, my parents had taught me early on that denominations were our extended family. While we may not agree with everything they believe, we should allow others room to be wrong. Just kidding. My mother taught me two levels of theology. One was Jesus, and the other was everything else. In the grand scheme of things, everything else doesn't matter because, in essence, only Jesus matters. So, I walked across the highway to the church, not even bothering to check what denomination it was because it was a dry place.

A black gentleman opened the door and took one look at me,

"You want some hot coffee and a towel? My name is T."

"I would love some."

I am from the South. Though I don't love coffee, sounding pleasant and appreciative is a necessary part of social communication. I was cold and thankful for the kindness. I had not been shown much kindness recently and yearned for positive human interaction. So, thinking T would pour me a cup of coffee already made me feel warm inside.

Following him into the kitchen, I realized I was more special to him than I thought as he dug out the coffee maker, coffee, filters, sugar, and cream and began finding me a clean towel. He hadn't offered me a cup of coffee already made. He made a pot of coffee only for me.

Sometimes, I can be obtuse, but God's graciousness, exhibited through His servant T's compassion, did not escape my notice.

"Are you hungry?" He asked. "I'm sure you are. Church is about to start. If you want to hang around, I'll hook you up. Make yourself at home." Then, not wanting to be late, T strode to the worship center.

As I sat in the entry area of the church, drying my hair and drinking my coffee, the tears began to flow. My feet already hurt. I was wet. Cold and miserable, T told me to make myself at home in God's house. Hard-headed, stubborn, and strong-willed, my heavenly Father still sent me a message here–I was at home in His house.

I finished my coffee and eased into the service. T wasn't visible. The truth is nobody was. Three months earlier, someone had been so kind as to shatter my glasses into a million pieces—while breaking some bones and giving me a concussion.

I eased into a pew and joined in the service. The praise and worship portion continued to bring quiet tears to my eyes.

Then, I discovered the pastor was not speaking. They had a guest. He was a missionary to Central America. That may not mean anything to you, but my mother spent her last many years dedicated to mission work. While serving all over the world, her second language was Spanish. The most significant portion of her work was in Central and South America. "Coincidences are God's way of showing He is in control," reads one of my favorite bumper stickers. It comforted me to hear the speaker's scripture reading in Spanish and his anecdotes from that region of the world.

"You're still here." Not a question in surprise. Just a simple comment made with pleasure.

T corralled me toward the back of the church. He introduced me to his wife, and they began to find some food in the church's mission pantry. Mrs. T loaded a bag down, and I almost asked about a backpack when T rounded the corner, took one look, and disappeared—only to reappear with a pack and cans with easy-open lids. No requests by me—he gave me a U.S. Air Force backpack full of food—food completely accessible, with the pull of a ring tab, by a man walking down the road–me.

God's Grace. It's amazing. Someone should write a song about that.

I walked out of the Apostolic Tabernacle in Jonesboro, Georgia, with a stuffed backpack, sated belly, and full, yet lighter, spirit.

Wow! The rain had ceased while I was in the church service. Things weren't going gang-busters, but life had a better feel. Most coolest so far!

I walked across the highway and headed north into the now night-darkened sky. At a hundred yards north, give or take a few feet, it began to rain again. "Lord, I already told you I am not gonna curse you and die. Oh Lord, You're beautiful. Your face is all I seek. For when your eyes are on this child, your Grace abounds to me." I sang. I sang reverently, I might add.

I walked. It rained harder. I prayed. It rained more. I sang. I began to stumble. I dropped my useless hitchhiking thumb.

"Lord. Not tryin' to ask for too much, but nobody notices me, and I'm getting tired. I have walked a long way. I am not stopping 'til you tell me to, but I could use some help here."

Exhaustion poured over me. However, within 30 seconds of my plea, I saw bright lights shining on the US 19/41 emergency lane in front of me.

It was a MARTA bus. It pulled up beside me, and the door opened. I looked up at the bus driver, "Ma'am, I only have 83 cents to my name." My brother's $15 was already almost gone. "Get on this bus, you fool. It's raining," she said with a smile. Relief does not describe my physical, much less emotional, response.

God's mercy. Who am I? He cared enough to time a MARTA bus to arrive at my point of desperation. He cared enough to die, but He cares enough to live for us, too? And not just good folks, but losers like me. "Really, Father? Who am I?"

"Well, thank you, Lord. You are an awesome God." I threw up that quick prayer. I'm unsure if it was in sheer desperation for the walk to end or if I thought my travails were past. In my head, I knew how this would play out. An acquaintance had told me that Greyhound would ship me anywhere for free if I told them I was homeless. I was now inside the Atlanta transit system. Of course, I had only ridden a Marta train once or twice and had never been on a bus, but I knew now I would make it to Boston or L.A. without a hitch. (I still had no idea where I was headed).

It stopped raining. If it were only daytime, I was sure the sun would have shone brightly and the bluebirds singing, "Zip-a-dee-doo-dah, Zip-a-dee-ay"…. the bus dropped me off at the station, and I found there was no such thing as a transfer to the train was available. "Bump in the road. That's all this is." I stood in place for several minutes. I needed to board the train. To do that, I needed to pass through the turnstiles, which required money, a MARTA card, or something. I stared for a few minutes. I started to ask someone, but remembered my promise when up walked a MARTA employee who asked, "Do you need to get on the train?" Looking up, "Wow! God, you are on point!" I said yes and proceeded to wait for the train. I got on and got off. It was all over but the cryin'. The Greyhound bus station was before me. All I had to do was walk in, explain I was homeless, and they would give me a bus ticket to anywhere but where I was. WOO-HOOO!

Track 3: Perplexity and Peace

Perplexed = bewildered, confused, and disturbed by it!

I was there. My mind and spirit were experiencing everything my physical being was going through in a whole other dimension. My previous life was a mess. My current situation was confounding.

The people around me, my immediate needs, yes, and the storm itself were punctuating what was occurring inside me.

One cannot be at peace and be perplexed at the same time.

As God dealt with me, I began to have a peace I did not comprehend. As troubles assaulted me, I would find more peace infused by the Spirit. Puzzled that He could accomplish peace in my life, no matter the outward circumstances does not equal perplexed. The kind of peace He offers goes beyond explanation, yet it provided completeness I had never experienced.

While you may discover the Greyhound employees and the drug dealers within this piece, the most consistent theme of this composition is that out of the dissonance of chaos, the Lord can provide peace.

"I am leaving you with a gift–peace of heart and mind. And the peace I give is a gift the world cannot give, so don't be troubled or afraid."

John 14:27 (NLT)

****

"Sir, I don't believe Greyhound does that anymore, but you can talk to a supervisor," said an attendant. That was not a problem; I only needed to turn on the charm and use my God-given and well-trained tongue to my advantage.

"Sir, several agencies can help you. We are not one of them. And you need to leave," said the supervisor flatly. Talk about being shot down! Then, to add insult to injury, a security guy told me to go as I tried to adjust my backpack straps so I could leave. Wow! Crash and burn!

I replied, "Buddy, I just got out of the hospital. Give me a second."

"If you need an ambulance, go across the street. I'm sure the police will help. Now, out!"

There was no mercy here. I walked away, and drug dealers instantly accosted me, offering their wares. I fled. I got two blocks, and a flood fell from the sky. I say it like that because this wasn't rain in the ordinary sense. In Texas, they'd call it a "Gully-washer." In Georgia, "It's raining cats and dogs." If that were true, it'd have been cats the size of tigers and dogs with the size and ferocity of werewolves. In less than thirty seconds, water drenched me to the skin. I noticed moisture greedily attacking the top of my tightly tied work boots. I looked around for Noah and his ark nearby. Just kidding. Even if vision were possible without my glasses, I could not have seen past the sheet of water flowing earthward. I was breathing water in with every breath and choking on it. The wind whipped my umbrella out of my hand and negated its usefulness when I caught up to it. I managed about three miles in this, trying to go anywhere but the bottom of the water world I had apparently been teleported to by aliens disguised as Greyhound security guys. As I walked, I sang praises and prayed—anything that at least kept the air flowing out rather than water flowing into my mouth.

I attempted to prove to God that I would at least go through the motions, but I wasn't feeling it. No, really, I promise, I wasn't feeling anything but pain before I even had walked a mile. Then cold. Then, nothing, as hypothermia began to set in.

As I approached one intersection, the wind and rain came at me from the south. The next, it blew from the north. Front, back, and ever downward—seeking to grind me into the pavement. I do not exaggerate. From a purely objective standpoint, it was an awe-inspiring storm. I have worked in hurricanes that couldn't touch what I experienced that night.

"O Lord, you're Beautiful…." One foot in front of the other and occasionally, "Having done all to stand," I stood trying not to topple over. Finally, I stumbled into a MARTA train station. The trains were shut down for the night, but "Thank you, Father, for shelter from this maelstrom." I knew I was in bad shape. I had stopped shivering a while before. It was not a good medical sign. I curled up on the concrete platform and dozed off.

I awoke with a start. I heard voices around the corner. I didn't want any trouble with the police. I tried to stand and had to pull myself up with my hands. My legs did not want to cooperate. Not good. I wondered back out into the rain. I had to keep moving. A hundred feet from the train station, I saw a sign, "Emory," a hospital. I wandered into the emergency room and asked permission to sit briefly and get warm. "We're not supposed to let you, but you can sit for a few minutes." It was warm. I began to shiver again, and as if on cue, the receptionist told me my time was up. 15-20 minutes was all I was given. It was enough for now.

I walked on.

It rained on.

At last, the sun filtered through the darkness, and the rain began to ease up. I found a bench on the leeward side of a building. Exhausted, I slept for 15 or 20 minutes while early morning commuters rushed through wet streets, trying to survive one more day in their personal rat races.

I struggled to my feet and walked a few steps. "Lord. It's that time again. I know you know, but I must ask for some relief." Almost at the point of falling, I raised my eyes as I rounded a curve on the now heavily traveled surface street. The rain stopped. The sun came out. I waited for the "Ahhhh" of an angelic choir—right in front of me beneath the clearing sky was a Chick-fil-A.

"Wow! Lord, when you do it, you do it right!" Not only relief but a refuge as well. For you unfamiliar with the fast-food (fast-food not in name only) restaurant Chick-fil-A, it has Christ-centered compassion as a company policy.

I stumbled through the door and asked to speak to the manager. "I cannot be a customer today, but I desperately need to sit down." Without a second thought, the manager said, with a caring smile on his face and a gentle tone,

"Buddy, you can not only sit down; you are welcome to stay as long as you want. Anything you need, ask me."

"Just a place to sit down, and thank you." I found a corner, set my backpack down, collapsed on a chair, and immediately fell asleep.

Note to the world: What would most places of business do with a bedraggled, backpack-laden, and soaked man? They would not allow him to sleep in their business. Chick-fil-A has broken with typical business models. They are closed on Sundays—one of the most profitable days of the week for a restaurant. They give away food by the tons to needy people. They let sleeping, bedraggled, backpack-toting men sleep in their place of business, oh yeah, while the backpack leaves a four-foot diameter puddle of water on the floor. Yet, they are one of the most profitable and fastest-growing companies. For all the business model designers, I am sure you would not be able to plan for those results without putting God first.

I woke—somewhat embarrassed, over both sleeping and the puddle. I approached a young lady—college age, and I'm guessing — "May I have a mop so I can clean up my mess," I sheepishly asked while pointing at what looked like a miniature model of Skull Island in the dining area. Without thinking, she said, "Of course not, sir. You are our guest. I'll clean it up." Kindness in a given situation speaks volumes about the inner condition of the heart. This young woman was raised with Jesus first—taught through word and example by her parents and supervisors at work. Compassion- it felt so good to feel it in action. I might be a human, after all.

By no means was I fresh, but I felt better. I walked and came upon the Atlanta Cathedral, sitting beside Second Ponce De Leon Baptist Church. "Interesting," I thought. I had never been in the Atlanta Cathedral. I am not Catholic, but I have long admired the construction of Catholic cathedrals and have had the opportunity to visit a few of them. I walked into the building. It was indeed beautiful. A certain serenity allows for good meditation in a beautiful, well-built sanctuary, and this one qualified. I saw no one, and I sat for a moment and meditated. I felt at ease. It was a good feeling.

I saw no piano. I have a slight piano dysfunction. I love to play, though I play primarily for myself—even when playing for others. It is an authentic, sane, and legal escape. I intentionally seek out pianos in a house, church, mall—pretty much anywhere. I wandered around, walked outside, and enjoyed the prayer garden.

One thing I knew for sure. The Baptist church next door would not have one piano—it would have several. I walked in. "May I help you," a voice rang out from somewhere. Finally, zeroing in on the source, I turned to the right and saw the friendly face matching the voice. "I was next door and enjoyed seeing the Cathedral's sanctuary." "Well, would you like to see ours?" she asked—as if sanctuary and worship center inspectors showed up every day at her door, blown in from a recent sky-destroying storm and looking road-worn and soaked. "Sure!" "Just go right up those stairs and through the door."

"Thanks."

I walked into the worship center. I might be bold—some would say brash or, at the very least, brazen, but I respected the apparent history of the church and did not sit down at the piano. I wasn't even going to ask. Looking down at myself and imagining how I must appear, I could not drum up the confidence to ask. No sane person who cared about a good instrument would've ever allowed me in my current condition to sit down at that piano.

Walking past the office, I yelled a quick thanks and proceeded to the door.

"Sir! Sir! Wouldn't you like to speak to someone?" I heard behind me. I backtracked to the office door. I answered affirmatively and sat down on a nice soft chair. The wait wasn't long.

"Hi. I'm David Hull."

"David Riordan, here. I think I may be able to remember your first name, although sometimes, I forget my own name."

He chuckled at my not-so-funny self-deprecation as if he knew what I meant through personal experience. I continue to be amazed at the compassion of some people who acted as if nothing was unusual about my appearance or how I showed up at their door. I liked this guy. I felt comfortable.

"So, what's happening in your life that brings you here?" Trusting him without hesitation, I launched into the short version you've already read. He listened attentively—never interrupting—and, without openly passing judgment, said, “I don’t know how you will make it to where you are going; I can’t do anything for you except pray with you.” “That’d be great,” I replied. He prayed. I left.

As I walked away, “Come on, Lord. This was a great place. You could have really helped me out. I am exhausted. I need some help. This church is capable. What’s the deal? I do appreciate the prayer and all. Don’t get me wrong, but is this guy just out of tune or what?”

I felt the presence of a Fatherly frown.

“Okay, okay, okay, but this was an opportunity for you to shine.”

Frown deepens. “Nothing is wrong with my ‘shine’ or what David did. Unlike somebody with whom I’m quite familiar, he knows how to follow directions. I have something better ahead.”

“I am thankful, Lord, and you noticed, I hope, I did not ask for anything.”

“You win a gold star. If I remember correctly, this was a multi-part agreement, and I, unlike somebody else, do not forget my agreements. You are supposed to be as thankful when I say no as when I spoil you with blessings.”

“I’m trying.”

“No try, just do.”

“Father. Come on now. Stealing lines from George Lucas? Really?”

“Silence, David, before you get yourself into a real pickle with me! I don’t steal. I don’t have to steal. Everything belongs to me anyway. Who do you think gave the genius to George to create Yoda, much less write the lines? I'm not doing 40 chapters of Job with you. Been there; done that; had it written; go read it."

"Sorry. I didn't mean 'steal' steal. Just trying to be funny."

"I'm not laughing, and I'm well aware of what you were trying to do. Don't push it."

"I am sorry."

"Get past it. I have."

"Thanks."

"Thanks for remembering to say thanks. Your mother taught you well."

He continued, "Now, think about baking bread. Before you have that great house-filling scent and then eat it, the dough must be kneaded and put in the oven. I am the Baker, and you are the dough. I have not yet completed the kneading process, and you're not yet smelling very good—trust me on that one—though the rain is helping. But, as you have told many people, 'To get through it, you gotta go through it.' So, get back to your journey. I have some kneading to do."

Track 4: Gardener

He goes by many names, and a rose by any other name remains the same.

The Potter, the Carpenter, the Fisher of Men, the Good Shepherd, and, of course, the Baker—whatever role He needs to play to reach us reveals His true identity, for God is Love.

From the plant being uprooted to the dough being kneaded, change is often painful and never comfortable.

Something had to pass away for me to change and to reach the point of life-altering faith; as some may say, “God had to take me down through there!”

When cooking, sugar is just sugar until it reaches about 236 degrees F. Then, something almost magical happens as the sugar molecules realign. It arrives at the softball stage, and grainy sugar becomes smooth, creamy fudge.

With heat and a few other ingredients, sugar becomes icing for a cake.

By this point in my story, I was being mixed, and I needed a few more ingredients and the heat. God provided them as only He can.

“Now, if anyone is enfolded into Christ, he has become an entirely new creation. All that is related to the old order has vanished. Behold, everything is fresh and new.”

2 Corinthians 5:17 (TPT)

****

The misery of each step set back in. My feet were getting in worse and worse shape. Wet boots and wet socks were not helping. Then, another well-timed blessing. Another church. I was bound and determined to keep my word, but I could not take many more steps, and staying in touch with God’s people was not breaking the promise of not asking. The door was open. "Thank you, Lord." Through the door, I trudged, shuffled, or stumbled—I can't decide what I would call my gait at that point.

"How may I help you?" spoke the receptionist. Then, of its own accord, my tongue blurted, "A dry pair of socks would be awesome."

"You idiot," I thought, "There may be no question mark after it, but that is asking—no getting around it." I am one of my worst judges and critics.

"Do you have a picture I.D.?"

"Picture I.D.? You gotta be kidding," I thought. "No, Ma'am." Before my mind launched into a silent, resentful diatribe, she said, "I think maybe we can help you with some socks at least, although next time you stop in, you'll have to have a picture I.D. Have a seat, and let me see what I can do."

A few minutes later, another woman came through the door carrying a bag. "Will any of these will work for you." Oh, my Lord! I don't think I had ever seen such a blessed sight. It was a whole bag of socks—dry socks, at that! If you've ever walked on "dish-pan" feet, you can relate. She told me to take as many pairs as I needed. I sat chagrined. "Lord, I broke my promise, yet you give me more than I asked for. You are indeed an awesome God!

"Now, in this bag," as she produced a second bag, "is a little food and a MARTA pass, so maybe you can be off your feet for a few minutes while you ride to wherever you're going."

No words can describe my embarrassment as I stood before my Lord. I hung my head. She said, "It is starting to rain again. You sit here as long as you need to and stay dry. I'll get you an umbrella." She gave me a fresh umbrella to replace the one torn by the wind during the previous night. Then she looked me in the eye and said, "We don't do this, but I want you to have this," as she slipped a folded 20 into my hand.

Wow. When would I ever learn that God would take care of me? When would I open my stubborn eyes and recognize the truth? All I could do was say thanks through choked, heartfelt tears and head out the door of what I discovered after the fact was Peachtree Road United Methodist Church.

I headed to the nearest bus stop. Riding—not walking is healing in and of itself. It is also a lot quicker. Before I realized it, I was on a train—then, another bus taking me further north.

While I had not forgotten our Father still had some kneading to do, once again, I fell into the trap of feeling like everything was worked out.

Easy rider.

As the bus went further north into Gwinnett County, I drifted into a conversation with an older man. I was becoming aware that God had placed me in the path of certain people for specific reasons. The first had been the African-American young man in Henry County. Now, I was face-to-face with another appointment.

As before, God's wealth of information began to flow through me. This man began to explain how he had been delving into science to find the meaning of life. What he had been delving into was mysticism in the guise of intelli-speak. In this day and age, the world has begun to mistake science for whatever some scientist says. One of the great minds of science who passed away, Stephen Hawking, is guilty of helping along this new-fangled religion by not clarifying the difference between science, as determined by the scientific method, and pseudo-science, as determined by whatever passes the lips of a well-thought-of intelligent man.

This older man, with whom I was discussing the meaning of life, had gone down every imaginable philosophical pseudo-scientific road. I listened as the bus we were on reached its apex and began its trip back south, but I was not about to walk away from a God-timed appointment. He believed in God, but there was no way we could know him. He felt the mental world in which we live and out of which we view our existence is determined by our confused minds, thus eliminating our ability to contact the Almighty.

"Fascinating point of view!" I stated. "I agree with everything you have just said." You might have pushed him over with a feather. "I believe that you are right—with a stipulation. We have lost our ability to contact God through our own doing. We increasingly confuse ourselves with every passing day, but I also believe the answer is much simpler than we realize."

I had his attention now. This was a man on a search who had reached a fitting conclusion. On our own, we are desperately lost and without hope. We can have the brightest minds of our generation seeking the truth and miss it by the entire cosmos. That lost.

"You see, I, like you, believe in God. There must be God. The Second Law of Thermodynamics says everything runs down and cannot be salvaged after a certain point. Entropy rules everything. That being the case, there is a definite end of things." I had his rapt attention now. "If a definite end exists, there had to be a beginning to this creation." He responded, "I haven't had a problem with that so far."

"Well, it is pretty obvious—and not trying to be simplistic—the answer is simple. If we cannot bridge the gap between our Creator and ourselves, He can." Before he could interrupt, I continued, "If the Creator is so powerful that He made the intricacy we can see in cellular structure and the vastness of the cosmos, don't you think managing to find a way to communicate with little old us would be easy?"

Dumbfounded, the man stared at me—having never considered the Almighty might consider talking to us inferior beings. "In fact," I said, "I would venture your opinion of the human race is about where it should be. We have misused and abused His creation. We have spit in His face, but like any father, He loves his children anyway. Love, my friend, is what you have left out of your God-equation. I believe He loves us enough that He was willing to become a man and prove it—thus bridging the communication and knowledge gap between us and Him."

I continued to explain the answer was that easy. It is the simplicity of love with the complexity of God's Grace. As an uninformed person cannot understand how a road is built, he can drive down it. God paved the path with love. We may not understand everything it took to make the path because the reasons may be like the complex road equipment used to construct our roads—beyond our perception until we learn some facts. The lack of knowledge, nevertheless, does not hamper our travels.

"And if you don't believe me, ask Him. If God is powerful enough to create this complexity, He is powerful enough to answer your questions. All you have to do is ask Him. He is powerful enough to hear your voice and distinguish your questions from mine. After all, I have questions I ask Him, and He is busy answering mine right now, but He can handle the load of all of us. He's God."

As we talked, we reached his stop and disembarked. He wanted to go home and continue our conversation, and I looked up to discover a Chick-fil-A right in front of the bus stop. Somehow, I knew another timely appointment was awaiting me inside. I told him he had heard what I had to say. But, his real answers would come from our Creator. "Go home and ask Him. I am sure He will answer."

Track 5: Walk of Faith

What is faith? And, better yet, what is the walk of faith? Faith begins and ends with God. It is the sure knowledge God will walk beside us in our journeys.

Early in my walk, I proclaimed to the young man in Henry County that I was stepping out on faith. That's what I wanted.

It was a crisis of faith. I needed what I did not have.

I had given up on the idea that I could achieve anything significant.

I called out to God. He had answered.

Substance and evidence build our faith. It was through His answer that I began to gain it.

God had begun to deal with me several days earlier, first through a Sergeant of the Spelding County Sheriff's Department and then through my brother.

The beginning of God's call was in a way I could understand—through others. That initial contact drew me closer to an understanding that I needed to reach out to Him. I saw God at work in and through others. It became a compelling drive to experience God the way they did.

In this piece, God's call starts a process, and the journey commences. There are highs and lows. These are the building blocks of faith. In the beginning, God is enigmatic. We experience Him, get to know Him, and the mystery fades as our faith grows. Then the Spirit speaks again, the mystery reconstitutes, and God calls us down yet more unknown roads. We may not know what lies down the paths we travel, but in knowing God, we know He goes before us.

Crises averted.

The old saying, "Seeing is believing," gives rise to another old expression, "blind belief." Seeing may be believing, but faith is more than seeing. It is more than belief. Faith is knowing, though it has not happened yet.

Our eyes may be fooled, but God-birthed faith cannot be.

"You see, in the good news, God's restorative justice is revealed. And as we will see, it begins and ends in faith. As the scripture declares, 'By faith, the just will obtain life.'"

Romans 1:17 (VOICE)

18

Out of the Oven

Woo-hoo! I had that $20 bill, and affording Chick-fil-A this time was doable. I was a customer! I walked to the counter, ordered, sat at the only empty table, and bit into one of the best chicken sandwiches I had ever eaten. "Man, this is good! Those waffle fries will be good in a moment." My mother labeled me early in life a "Lazy-Susan" eater. You've seen them—those large round serving plates that sit in the middle of the table. You can spin them around and take portions of different items for yourself. I eat one thing at a time and then turn my plate to the next food. I don't mix up my servings, either. Why spoil one great taste by getting the juice of something else on it? While considering a "Lazy-Suzy" eating faux pas, testing a waffle fry before finishing my sandwich, I noticed a smiling face on the opposite side of the table.

I do not have the foggiest human conclusion as to why Sally decided to stop at my table. It was a God-thing. No other explanation makes sense. I was not the only person eating alone or with a backpack. I wasn't the roughest-looking person in the joint. I had been relatively dry for hours and did not look wholly bedraggled. I may have looked tired, but I don't think I was any more noticeable than anyone else. It was a God-timed appointment.

"How are you today?" she asked. "It's been a long day for me," I responded, explaining that I was on a faith journey. We then launched into a conversation about faith and hope. I explained we do not base biblical faith and hope on some 'pie in the sky' flimsy feelings. "Now faith is the substance of things hoped for, the evidence of things not seen," I quoted from Hebrews 11:1 in the New Testament. "Substance and evidence. It's amazing how we have lost our ability to dissect an English sentence. Prepositional phrases modify a specific noun. In this case, the nouns are substance and evidence, yet we seem distracted by the 'things hoped for and things not seen.' Those are modifiers and not the point or subject. The nouns are substance and evidence, so faith is substance and evidence—not some wispy, limp-handed, 'Gee, I guess it might be sort of possible' kind of feeling. Faith is hard-core, certain knowledge that something will happen—even though it has not happened yet. We exercise faith when we step on a concrete sidewalk on which we have never stepped. Why? Because we have walked on concrete before, and it has not failed us. That is faith: knowing my Father will care for me because He has done it repeatedly. He goes before me in all things. I know this. I do not doubt He will continue because He has never failed me."

Sally looked at me as I wrapped up my mini-sermon. She said, "Now, David, you will believe me when I tell you this, but nobody else would. I lead a discipleship group of younger women that meets on Monday night—here in just a few hours. You come here on a 'faith journey' and launch into this conversation about faith and hope. The curriculum for the discipleship training was written months ago. The time frame was determined months ago when we started this study. The topic of tonight's study is 'Faith and Hope.' It is staggering to believe God cares enough to send you through this door when I needed to hear what you had to say to share it with these young ladies."

I replied, "No. What's staggering is that God would use an individual in whom everyone has lost hope to deliver the message you needed to hear. Staggering and humbling." I had to blow my nose and dry my eyes.

When I returned to the table, the restaurant manager had returned the money I had spent on my meal, and a cashier, I believe, had paid for two more sandwiches to take with me. Sally had been sharing my story.

I must take a moment and speak about this restaurant chain again. They break "sound business practices" every day. They give and give. No one complained that Sally stood beside and then sat at my table to talk with me. No one griped that the company and individual employees provided my meal and then food for the road. If I had my guess, if corporate Chick-fil-A found out, it would praise them for their actions. The company elevates such for being Ambassadors of Christ. They are fearless in their stance of compassion for others. I have seen it firsthand, and in this time of being kneaded by the Master Baker, they were who

God used to give me relief when I sorely needed it earlier—and later in this part of my story. (Yes, you'll hear about this company again.) At this point, Chick-fil-A was God's sanctuary, where a washed-up man delivered a message of faith and hope to a lady who needed it. God uses people and companies who make themselves available in mighty ways. God, not coincidence, in a state with over 250 Chick-fil-A restaurants, in a metropolitan area of nearly 6 million people, in a restaurant with, and I'm guessing, 50-75 employees—at a bus stop beyond where I intended to disembark—brought together one broken man with one active servant to deliver a poignant illustration and message to a group of young women in a course of study designed months earlier for that specific night. Call it a coincidence if you want. I'll call that God's way of getting a message across. On this, I need to say no more.

Sally returned to my table, said she was leaving, and would give me a ride to the next exit—if I was interested. Of course, I was. At this point, a woman who had never met this hitch-hiking, homeless man brandished her weapon of personal protection—a plastic knife. We laughed. We both knew what and who protected her! She dropped me off, and we said our goodbyes, and I proceeded to try to find a ride.

Not long after Sally dropped me off, I walked to the entrance ramp of I-85. A young man pulled up and picked me up. "I'm only going up one exit," he told me.

"God-appointment," read the neon light, which, in my imagination, lit up the sky.

I hopped in without hesitation. This was getting pretty awesome. God could and would use me. It was also emotionally exhausting—considering I was an emotional wreck already. In the next ten minutes, he proceeded to pour out his story. He was facing a potential 25-year prison sentence on the following day. He had rented the van he was driving to move all his stuff from the apartment he had been living in. Drugs, friends, and a former employer had led him down a path that only Christ might pull him off. I prayed for him.

He did not want to part company. I have been there, where any friendly face was better than no face. Fear of what might happen the following day in court weighed heavily upon his whole being. He, however, had a time constraint with the van, and I had to keep moving.

Onward and upward. Thumb out—or back to ignored thumb out. It was a palpable sensation. I suddenly felt a change. I had no impending appointments. It seemed nobody saw me. While I was not invisible, God did not want me to be seen. It was back to learning time.

I walked into a Walmart. I slept for a few minutes on a bench. I had become so unnoticeable that local cops, Walmart employees, passersby—nobody noticed me. An overwhelming sense of being alone encased me. I may as well have been Matt Damon stranded on Mars. I was a million miles from nowhere. All alone—yet still in Metro Atlanta.

With a sinking, desperate feeling, I realized my ride had taken I-985, and while I was still going north, it was a northern path that would not take me any great distances. I remembered this exit shared a hotspot destination with an off-ramp from I-85, one of the largest malls in the world. So, all I had to do was walk toward I-85. It couldn't be too far out of the way. It probably isn't—if you're in a car—if you don't make a wrong turn—if it doesn't resume raining.

Track 6: The Cross

It all comes down to crosses--His and ours.

My journey had finally brought me to that pivotal moment—the excising of the final part of me, or at least who I thought I was.

The truth is, I never had an identity. I never knew who I was meant to be. My best attempts in life had left me trying to fill the empty holes with cheap substitutes: work, knowledge, drugs, and trying to play the hero. The latter was a desperate effort to rescue another because I could not save myself.

With all of the success I previously had in life, the truth is I was a failure. When I could not find solace in pursuing knowledge and career success, I collapsed into addiction. When I could no longer pursue that obsession, I tried to help another, ending in a resounding failure that almost cost me my life.

I had to die, but not in the way those people had tried to take my life, and not from a heart attack like the one I had suffered only a few days earlier. No, I had to follow the example set before me by Christ. I had to nail my old life to a cross.

Dying is a frightening thought. Knowing there is life on the other side in no way lessens the fear, for I didn't know what it was like to live that way. All I knew was what I had been doing wasn't working.

"We know that our old self was crucified with Him in order that the body of sin might be brought to nothing so that we would no longer be enslaved to sin. So, you must consider yourselves dead to sin and alive to God in Christ Jesus."

Romans 6:6,11 (ESV)

****

At one point, soaking wet feet in unbearable pain, my mind beginning to lose a grip on reality from hypothermia, and my chest pounding in agony; I collapsed against a guard rail and slumped onto the ground. Even to my tortured mind, it was clear that the mall had just closed as hundreds of cars passed by my nearly unconscious body, lying in the mud. Desperation and fear seized my mind,

"Not yet, Lord. Not here—not now—not alone!"

"Son, I am not done with you yet. They will not see you. They will not stop. Your dependence must be on Me and Me alone. It is a hard thing you are going through. I know! I made you, and I realize your limits better than you do! But, if you want to get through this, you've got to go through this. Sound familiar?"

"But Lord, I can't take anymore!" I sobbed in anger and fear.

"I understand your breaking point better than you do. I love you, but for me to use you, you must lose you, for 'whoever loses his life for My sake will find it.' It can no longer be about you. It has to be about me. That is your purpose. Only in finding and living out your purpose will you ever find My peace that passes all understanding. That is where you will find sanity and security in this crazy world you all are making out of what I created. David, I have plans for you, plans for you to prosper. I don't want you to fail. I need you to be at full strength, which is My strength. You are rediscovering you have the keys to my bank of wisdom—even when you are spiritually bankrupt. You also have the keys to my strength, even when you have none left—and you have anything and everything else you'll need for which I created you. Stop fighting Me! I AM the answer you crave. You know this—you are my child. When will you let Me be your total fulfillment? Whenever you are ready, arise, make the pack lighter—you don't need everything in it, and with every step you take tonight, I'll give you the strength you need—no more and no less. I am telling you upfront because I don't want you to stop. I have another appointment for you. Don't worry. Whether each step feels like your last, you'll have what you need to take another—one step at a time. Your appointment is waiting. Now, no questions—hop up when you're ready to depend totally on me."

I lay in pain—not believing what God was telling me. All my focus was on the pain in my chest, my inability to catch my breath, the agony in my feet, and the agony of my mind. Finally, having no choice other than lying in the mud, I began putting my hands under me, having no clue how I would stand. When I got my hands under me, I got a knee up, and while I did not understand how I'd draw another breath, I could take another at the end of each. This was not taking one day but one second at a time. I managed to stand. I looked the way I had come and saw my backpack in the middle of the sidewalk 50 feet back—my umbrella 50 feet beyond that (inexplicably not being blown by the wind). Remembering what my Father had told me, I unloaded five or six cans of baked beans and a couple of other items—making a noticeable stack a potential needy person might find. Putting on the backpack was doable.

I began to walk once more into another fomenting torrential downpour. Interesting word, foment. The archaic meaning: "to bathe in warm or medicated lotions." Nothing felt warm about the rain, yet I warmed with each step. Nothing felt medicating about any drop falling from the sky that night, and a lot fell; however, I felt bathed in some secret medicine that would ultimately bring healing.

I walked alternately with the umbrella pointed straight ahead or behind, depending on which direction the rain switched to, but it pummeled me horizontally for hours. Cars rode by and splashed me. Miles fled beneath my feet until I finally came to I-85. Well, I arrived at a bridge passing over I-85—no exit or entrance ramp here. I walked on, hoping to find a frontage road. It wasn't happening. A bit further, I saw cars turning to the left at a light. That had to be it. Thank you, Lord.

I turned left and walked into a subdivision with no apparent exit. I intelligently concluded one way in, one way out because I walked to the back of the subdivision where some new construction was. There was no way out, no way out legally, that is. I stumbled through the mud of a job site and into a right-of-way that cut back to I-85.

"Well, the police may stop me for walking on an interstate—if they can see me, but there's little chance in this rain." So I climbed over the guard rail and walked. Within ½ mile, I saw a sign, "Hamilton Mill Parkway 1 Mile."

Just when I thought I would mount a celebration party, an eighteen-wheeler zoomed past me, giving me a bath from a rainwater-filled puddle. I stepped to the side quickly and found my left leg knee-deep in a water-filled hole. As I fell forward, my left forearm slammed into heavy equipment parked along the roadside, resulting in more pain. I put my good arm underneath me and had the strength to stand.

"Lord, you are amazing. I would have bet my last dollar I would not be able to take another step, yet, 10 miles on, injured and blinded by wind and rain, I find it okay to keep walking. Thank you for being true to your word."

"It's my way of showing my love for you. Anything less, and you'd have died. If you had stopped, you'd probably have died—you would have certainly stepped back out of my will and plans for you."

"Died? I would have died?"

"You did not stop, though; I am not a knower of things that don't happen."

"That actually makes sense."

"I always make sense. It's not me—it's you." He continued, "Without my strength, you are finished. How's that for no choice—or not much of a choice? That will be your only choice for the rest of your life, My way or no way. I'll be sure to let you know when you start to stray. I assure you that you will not be given as much latitude as I have given before. I have plans, and you are getting older. I want you to prosper. I want the world to recognize what 'I AM' can do with a washed-up old drug addict—a believer who has life-altering faith. I have plans specifically for you. So, don't let yourself and Me down anymore."

"I'll do my best, Lord."

"I know you will because any step without Me will be without My strength. You know how it feels now to walk physically through My strength. Next, you must transfer the knowledge into spiritual things. Now, I think you have a little way to go before you get there."

As I stood a little straighter, I looked down at my arm. It was swelling. There was no question in my mind; I knew a broken bone when I saw one.

I walked the mile in reasonably good spirits. I climbed the exit ramp and discovered—to my pleasant surprise—a QT gas station. I went straight to the bathroom and worked at removing my boots. The boots were the easy part. It was the socks that were the problem. The injured "dish-panned" skin of my feet was sticking to my socks. I cried out in pain as I removed the offending socks. I was glad it was the middle of the night, and no one else was around. It took me an agonizing 15 minutes or so of changing my socks before I realized my left arm didn't hurt. Before I could even say anything, He said, "My Grace is Sufficient, and I will not let too much happen that I don't provide a way of escape even if it's 'on my dime,' so to speak. It's always on my dime." I want you to recognize where it is coming from."

"Thank you, Lord!"

"That, son, is one way of recognizing where it comes from. Obedience is another."

"What do I do now?"

"Do what comes next, listen for my voice, and watch for my direction."

Walking up to the counter, I said, "Hi. I am kinda stranded. I have money to eat but need to dry out and stay warm. Do you mind if I hang out for a few?" The QT employee smiled, "Listen, I used to work at a gas station where homeless people always hung out. It doesn't bother me any. Just don't do anything sketchy, and you can hang out as long as you want." It was a bolt of lightning moment as I realized I had been labeled homeless. It hurts the first time. "Thanks," I said as I got myself a cup of coffee.

Two appointments took place that night. One was a gentleman who had warrants for his arrest. He was tired of running. He was about to call the cops on himself. He decided to hang out for a while as well. We talked about the difference Christ could make in his life.

The second was a nurse named John. He prayed for me.

Being confessedly homeless, I did the shelterless thing—got two large trash bags and slept in their cover from the rain behind the QT.

Two hours later, I crawled out of my trash bags and walked back around the front. The young man with warrants was gone, and it was time for me to leave. The manager had arrived for the morning.

I left—heading straight down the street to where I had been told was a rather large church. "Do what comes next and listen, huh? Lord, I am doing what comes next, and you keep giving me the strength I cannot claim in any shape, form, or fashion as my own..."

Laaaaaaaadies and gentlemen! Let me direct your attention to the center ring. The Amazing Idiot is here for your viewing pleasure. Look as God blesses him with a certifiable string of miracles and watch him complain.

Well, for your information, it never got that far because it expended too much energy to complain, and I was beginning to understand. He wanted me to dwell in the moment and appreciate each one. I had no choice. Is it starting to sound familiar? It is a shame to be as certifiably intelligent as I am and as stupid—sometimes—not always. I was living on the edge—not of the past year, but the precipice of now.

Choose life or death. With Him = life and life more abundantly. Without Him = death for me or something I am coming to understand as much worse than that.

I shoved the complaints back down my throat, "O Lord, you're beautiful. Your face is all I seek…. Lord, I am sorry I keep singing the same song. It just reminds me to seek you."

"Sorry? Look, son, I am the one who created creatures who sing 'Holy, Holy, Holy' day and night for eternity. You have to understand those words change every time you sing them. You are growing, and I hear new, deeper, and greater praise with each growth spurt. What may sound like monotony to you is an endlessly changing blessing of praise to Me. You hear with your ears, which is one of the ways you only 'know in part,' for one day, you'll know things even as I do. When you sing your simple melodies, I hear a symphony of spiritual quality that changes as you grow. There is so much more to this creation than you all will ever discover, and it brings glory and honor to Me, but I made it for you. That's how special you are to Me."

"Thanks, Lord. You are awesome. Now, where is that church? The dude said it was only ½ a mile down this road. I got to have walked more than that."

"Keep walking."

I walked. I came to a red light at the end of a community park. A man pulled up to the light. I walked towards his open window to ask where this church was. He hurriedly rolled his window up and looked in the other direction. He raced off when the light changed.

Disconcerted, I walked towards another vehicle stopped at the red light but across the street. You would have thought I was the pilot of a 747, and she was air traffic control without the flashlights. Back and forth from capital X to Y as she motioned me away. “All I needed were directions. A little kindness and compassion would go a long way!” I shouted at the top of my lungs. She heard me, as did the drivers in the three cars behind her.

“Your anger is justified if not inexpertly displayed.”

“I hear you, Lord. What would you have me do—sit down, weave a whip, and turn over some tables?”

“Now, son, that worked for Me—probably wouldn’t do you much good in this situation. I’ll choose to ignore your sarcasm. One of these days, you will learn to appreciate Me. My advice—though not command, is to use the anger to solve something other than simply venting.”

“I am listening.”

“Now, keep walking.”

I did walk—back the way from which I had come. I had seen a store a quarter mile before and decided to ask for directions, and my Father did not stop me. “Yeah, buddy, the church you’re looking for is just past the light.” Of course—past the light where I had already been.

I arrived at an empty parking lot. It was only about 7 a.m. I sat down in a little café style area the church had out front and dozed. I awoke—still nobody.

I walked next door to the animal hospital I had passed. “Do y’all know anything about this church next door?” I asked the receptionist. “Not really. I see people in the parking lot from time to time. A lot of them on Sundays.”

I walked past the church. Then, looking down the hill at a graveyard and feeling full of myself, I quipped, "Well, Lord, I found the church. They're all here." I saw a sign that read "Church Members Only," and arriving at a sign that said "Open on Sundays," I wrote a note asking, "What about Monday-Saturday?" I left it on the marquee.

"That, at least, is closer to getting some kind of result. Come on, Dave, don't stir up strife if you won't be here to help make a change."

I walked back up the hill feeling quite the comedian. I dozed back off. Waking, now thoroughly frustrated, I noticed a slew of cars parked behind the animal hospital. I was feeling now not like a comedian but like a fool. OMG! The church's offices must be up the hill and beyond sight. Behind the hospital, I walked. No offices. Nothing but parked cars with the former occupants now engaged in exercise in the health club beside the animal hospital.

Tired, frustrated, and unsure what to do, I walked into The Bodyplex. "May I help you?" came the compassionate and concerned inquiry from the lady at the desk. "Do you know anything about the church next door?"

"Not much, but you need some assistance."

This lady dialed the phone without batting an eyelash, looking down her nose at me, or anything negative.

Sitting near the counter on a comfortable lobby chair, I briefly explained what I had been going through. Finally, I told of my necessity to leave town.

When she asked me where I was headed, Boston was the only possibility that sprung to my lips—although I had toyed with a dozen locations.

Within a few minutes, kind people surrounded me. One gentleman went to his locker and retrieved dry socks and shoes. A few minutes later, a hot—you guessed it—Chick-fil-A meal came through the door, and as I was about to stand, a third person walked up and asked, "Didn't you say you were going to Boston?" "Yes," I replied. "Good—cause a friend is buying you a bus ticket."

I was dumbfounded. Several people who had never seen me before—one who still had not met me—had reached out to help me. "Miraculous?" you ask. Yes, because 15 minutes, either way and I would have missed the confluence of individuals that day. God is always on time. After being vetted by some professional policemen who treated me with the utmost respect and added nothing but kindness, I realized the kneading and baking were over. I felt like a warm loaf of bread.

"Lord. Thank you! You should have told me this appointment was for me!"

"Why do that and spoil all the fun? Go ahead. Call Me the Drama King if you like, but I do like showing off. I created you guys in a way that appreciates the extra effort involved in putting on a production. You are, after all, in My image. I want you to understand how precious you are to Me. Without the kneading and baking processes, how could you understand how cool it Is when I step into the picture? Plus, bread doesn't turn out right without being kneaded, and bread does not determine when it is ready. Bread doesn't understand what it needs, nor does it understand the oven's heat. You've got to agree with how good it smells when baked right by the baker. You, son, are a masterpiece. I am your Baker, and you are an awesome, sweet-smelling piece of work! That is spiritually speaking. You need a shower, but everything in its time."

"Oh Lord, you're beautiful,
Your face is all I seek,
For when your eyes are on this child
Your grace abounds to me
I want to take your word
and shine it all around
But first, help me to just live it, Lord
And when I'm doing well,
help me to never seek a crown
For my reward is giving glory to you
Oh Lord, please light the fire
That once burned bright and clear
Replace the lamp of my first love
That burns with holy fear."

"Now, that's a song from those lips worth hearing. It improves each time! Now, you have a trip and some things to do for Me. You're not where I want you yet. You still have some growing to do. I have some amazing things to show you. I have some healing to give you—and if you think the arm was something, wait'll you see what I can do with your heart and mind—if you'll let Me!"

19

Prepared to Serve

Having just been issued a nursely command to lie down, I took stock of my situation. This hospital, 90% closed, had been converted into an emergency-services-only facility by the state of Massachusetts. As I approached the building, its dark windows accentuated my feelings of loneliness—an absolute and conclusive separation from everything that had gone before.

Whatever might come, I did not know. Sheer exhaustion weighed upon me. I was a stumbling, bedraggled mess, my legs barely able to communicate the oversized entry—made to accommodate the world's injured.

Those two days in the storm had been an incredible time with God. The past two had been as fulfilling, but I was way beyond—beyond any point I'd ever been physically, emotionally, and spiritually. It was as if the first two days were an introduction to a new life. The second two had been more of a realization of what it all meant. This realization didn't change my current mess, nor did it imply I was suddenly a greater super-Christian. I was broken, but at least I recognized it, and, more importantly, now I knew in Whose strength I needed to remain.

It had also been a journey deep into unrequited and continued exhaustion. The profundity of my spiritual position was evident; however, so was the reality of my physical situation. Whether I would ever make it back to Georgia, I didn't have a clue. I needed clearness of thought to evaluate everything better. In my current state, the only thing clear was I was where I needed to be—in a hospital.

As I lay in the hospital bed, I began to ruminate over all I'd been through, equally questioning my spiritual and physical destinations.

Track 7: Hymn of Praise to the God Who Changes Hearts

"Agnus Dei," this song begins. Is He not the Servant of servants? "Behold the Lamb of God that taketh away the sin of the world," proclaimed John the Baptist. Indeed, our Lord serves us and motivates us to help others.

In my journey, there are two recurring themes. There are the God-appointments, where God sent me to an individual for a specific purpose. However, my brother loves me and noticed the moments God sent others to minister to me in my crisis.

In this journey of faith, God was working some things out in my life, but the call to serve others never dimmed. It is the same for others called out and set apart. Just as God had begun changing my heart, God had changed others before me. They were answering His call.

He is a God who makes all things new, And this Hymn is to honor Him for all the hearts He has turned towards me!

"A new heart also will I give you, and a new spirit will I put within you: and I will take away the stony heart out of your flesh, and I will give you a heart of flesh."

Ezekiel 36:26 (KJV)

****

Two days earlier:

I was supposed to have left the Greyhound bus depot near Gainesville, GA, at about 1:00 p.m. heading northward. The roofing contractor who had purchased the ticket for me at the Gwinnett County health club had also secured an Uber ride. I arrived about an hour early.

The Uber driver was another "God Appointment" arranged for me. As I write this nearly two years later, I had to pull out my notes scribbled on torn paper to remember her name. I may not have remembered Katherine's name, but I remember her impact on me.

An immigrant from a Caribbean island, she was standing on a firm foundation of her faith. Any Uber driver might have shown up, but I got one that fed me Godly encouragement for the forty-five-minute drive to the depot. The feeding was not only spiritual.

"You must be hungry," Katherine said.

"I won't deny it," I admitted.

"Come with me!" She boldly commanded as she headed towards the convenience store, doubling as a bus depot.

"Now, get what you want!"

Without question, anyone who knows me knows what I did. I headed straight to the back of the store, grabbed a cold Diet Coke, and returned to the front counter, where Katherine awaited me.

"No, no, no, no!" as she grabbed me, gently forcing me back into the depths of the store. "I said, 'Get something!'"

Reluctantly but gladly, I selected a Three Musketeers. She just shook her head and marched through the store, picking up a sandwich, chips, and a two-liter Diet Coke, putting the small bag of chips back, and grabbing a larger one. $9.35 later, she hugged me goodbye, leaving me with a five-dollar bill in my hands. "I'll be praying for you."

I would love to call Katherine an angel. She was undoubtedly my angel, but I don't want to take anything away from the woman. An angel could have been sent to minister to me. They are at God's beck and call. But, no, she was not an angel.

Katherine was a great example of how the Body of Christ should operate. Something cemented itself in me that day by God through Katherine that I continue to use as a guiding principle. In truth, we do not live in the past, nor do we live in the future. We live in the now, and God brings us opportunities to reach others at His pace, not ours. If we focus on the past or future, we will miss those God places in our paths today.

Waving out the car window and smiling broadly, Katherine hung a right out of the parking lot, leaving me with a bag full of food. I would be glad I had it to put with my backpack supplies. Variety is a good thing; however, that two-liter? It would be gone before the bus pulled away from my current perch.

It would be nine-and-a-half hours of waiting.

Meandering around the parking lot got old fast. I tried to strike up a conversation a time or two, and finally, I took a nap on the walkway alongside the building. Bored to tears, I cleaned the entire parking lot and surrounding grassy areas and took another nap.

I checked with the folks inside.

"Delay, delay, and delay," was all they told me.

I walked to the next parking lot. I wanted to write some notes for a minute in the Waffle House. I stayed until the restaurant filled with sheriff's deputies. Okay, maybe not "filled," per se, but two tables' worth and a couple at the bar. Too many for my comfort level. I was not yet out of Georgia. They did not make me feel safer. I nodded at the water-glass-filling waitress and slipped back out, heading whence I came.

And that was just the first hour!

Not really.

By this point, it was 7:30 p.m., and we finally had an ETA from Greyhound. The station owner proclaimed at my query,

"Your bus will be pulling in shortly. It should be here in the next thirty minutes."

I was not unhappy. The past two days may have been an incredible journey, for God had met me where

I was. He had spoken with me, touched me, and healed me. He had altered forever how I would walk with Him, but my journey in this life was far from over. Things like waiting on a Greyhound bus still had to take place. I was bone-weary. My body screamed at me, and I could not express how happy my feet were in new socks and shoes.

Returning to the side walkway, I scrambled around, gathering the socks I had laid out to dry. The sidewalk looked like a Christmas decoration littered with pink, green, and white socks drying in the early evening air. (By the way, I still have those pink and green furry socks. They are mementos of my time with God and of the kindness of others). I tied my still-wet boots to my backpack. I took the last swig from my Diet Coke, slung my pack on my back, adjusted my cap, and gazed expectantly toward the entry of the lot.

No matter how intently I looked at the entry, the bus wouldn't pull in. Shucking my backpack, it resumed its waitful stance beside me on the ground.

Grabbing a fresh cold Diet Coke from inside the store, I committed not to open it until after I was on the bus. Some commitments a man should never make! Slouching onto a bench, I returned to my "waiting mode."

9:30 p.m.: Light splashed excitedly across my visual cortex as extreme fatigue seemingly thinned the separation between the world and my brain. No matter the narrowing effect of the exhausted tunnel vision I was developing, no force could or would stop me from seeing and boarding the bus—including the exhaustion. The bus driver opened the door. I climbed aboard, found a seat, and waited patiently for the "Welcome to South Carolina" sign.

I never saw it! They don't put up those signs on backcountry border crossings. This bus made every podunk town stop on the road! I was only 30 minutes from the border, but it took 3 ½ hours before I heard the bus driver declare a specific stop—Something-Or-Another, South Carolina!

Passengers boarded, and passengers disembarked. I changed buses a couple of times. Minutes rolled into more minutes, and hours blurred into more hours. Darkness morphed into dawn, and before I realized it, night filled the bus again as I crossed into New Jersey.

"Ladies and Gentlemen, we are approaching New York City. If you have a connection to Boston, your route has been canceled due to a maintenance issue with that bus. There will be another bus leaving New York City for Boston at 6:30 in the morning."

Noooooo! Wow, I didn't think I could handle it, but then again, did I have a choice?

Exiting the bus inside the Port Authority Bus Terminal, I saw an LED display above the next bus dock. "Boston." I had an idea. The girl next to me seemed to have it at the same time. I grabbed one of her suitcases, and we made a mad dash to the ticket counter.

I let the girl go to the counter first, and almost immediately, the next attendant called me. The girl's attendant stepped away from the desk. Mine said,

"We just had two cancellations for that route, and we can swap out your ticket."

The girl was getting hers at the same time. Behind us was an ever-lengthening line consisting of our previous fellow riders. They had seen the LED sign moments too late. Sadly, they were not to be as fortunate as the girl and me.

Having an hour to burn, I spent it seeing the all-too-bright New York City lights around the station. Upon returning to the bus line, I discovered my bus had arrived and was loading. Once again, I was last in line. I allowed the girl to go in front of me. As I boarded behind her, she made for the only available seat near the bus's rear!

My whole inner being sank into a puddle beneath my feet. My heart may have even stopped for a second. I couldn't believe it. I had now been on the road since Sunday afternoon—seventy-eight hours! I left Georgia a wreck. I had not recouped in any way. If anything, I was worse off. It took everything I had to face the fact and turn around. It might be nine more hours before I left the Big Apple. The realization hit me like a wrecking ball to my soul.

Usually, I would have taken it in stride. I'd never spent more than a few hours in the City, which had been in the daylight. I was not well, and I was not in the right frame of mind. It didn't matter how bright the lights were; crushed, my spirit seemed to drift into a dark place.

I turned, heartbroken, to head back out of the bus with the realization I'd be in New York City for several more hours. Let's face it. I didn't have anywhere to go when I got to Boston. I'd talked to my friend, Danielle, on a borrowed phone while passing through Delaware. Staying with her was not an option, but that didn't matter. I just wanted the journey to be over.

As if by magic, the very front row had one available seat. I'd swear it hadn't been empty when I got on, but it sure was now! The relief was palpable. It was indescribable. It was awesome!! My seatmate moved his jacket, clearing the way for me to plop down. After twenty-four hours on a bus, who'd think I would be this relieved? You don't know.

"Hi. My name is Ahmed."

And with that, weariness drained away. My whole being invigorated, pain disappeared, my mind cleared, and my heart said, "God Appointment!"

Ahmed had grown up in the ghetto of the Bronx. Life had not been kind to him. He'd begun running drugs while still in elementary school. He hadn't finished high school before he graduated to prison. It is an all-too-common story repeated in the inner-city, gang-controlled ghettos.

"But I did everything right after that," he continued to tell me. "I got my GED in prison, and when I got out, I stayed away from the old gang. I stayed away from drugs. I didn't even drink! I got a real job, met my girl, had a baby, and married. I love my daughter. She means everything to me, but things went bad with my wife."

And now, we had arrived at the crux of the problem. Now, I saw why Ahmed was on a Greyhound headed to Connecticut.

"It got bad. I couldn't make enough money, and of all people, my girl wanted me to rejoin my old gang. The money's too good. I swore I'd never go back, and when I told her I wouldn't, she kicked me out of the apartment and moved some chump in."

Ouch! I could see the pain in his eyes as the light from the road bounced off them like flashing emergency lights from a frantic ambulance pinned in by rush-hour traffic. Desperation gripped him, pouring out unrelenting from his soul. I felt it as it washed out of him and over me. But, no matter how much he let out, it would only regenerate from within his broken heart in a never-ending stream of regret.

"It's not fair. What could I have done differently? I could not go back, but I don't know if I can go on! And now? Now she won't even let me see my daughter."

He continued, "I bought this ticket because if I stayed, I'd only end up in trouble!"

Ahmed's sister had managed to extricate herself from inner-city life. She had moved to Hartford and had a spare room. She was an oasis. He was desperate and looking for answers. He, at least, had somewhere to land.

He had a brush with Islam in prison. His mom had been a regular at the church he'd stopped attending as a child. He had heard of a dozen different religions but didn't know which way to turn or what to believe. He knew a God existed, for the world was too beautiful.

Ahmed talked for over an hour. I didn't interrupt. I didn't know what to say, but I intrinsically understood he needed to let it out. When he finished, words began to flow.

Softly, I said, "If what you say is true, and God exists because of everything you experience and understand, and if He's powerful enough to create everything, don'tcha think He's powerful enough to talk with you?"

"But why would He?"

Ah, then I understood. Battered and bruised throughout his life, with a recent injury punctuating his feelings of hopelessness, Ahmed didn't think he was worthy.

"Ahmed, I understand. You feel hopeless because you've screwed up in life and think you're not worth loving. But, brother, no matter how people may make you feel, don't confuse them with God. He created you. He loved you enough to become a man and give up His life for you, and He rose again, so you don't have to live like this. It's not that problems all disappear. But, he'll walk you through them all, and what may seem unbearable now will become victories in your life."

"How do I know this is true, that your Jesus is the answer?"

"That's the easy part. I won't sit here and beat you into submission until you believe. It is a rather simple thing and something I don't have to convince you. You know there's a God. It makes sense He can hear you. Talk to Him. He's perfectly able to deal with you in a way you can understand! Jesus made the way possible. Talk to God. He'll do the convincing. He will make Himself real to you."

Ahmed disembarked in Hartford, Connecticut.

I rolled into Boston at three in the morning. Nothing but stone benches awaited me for a place to rest my body, but it was enough. I crashed and burned—that is until the station came alive at about 5:00 a.m. with the morning commuter traffic.

Hopelessly roused, I wandered down the stairs and out onto the sidewalk. I was a bit overwhelmed. It seemed ages since my brother had handed me his last fifteen dollars, but it had only been four days.

"Lord? What am I supposed to do now?"

Downtown Boston is as intimidating as any large, unfamiliar city. I felt incredibly alone but safe for the first time in nearly a year. My disenfranchisement was almost complete with anyone in Georgia; however, I was in the middle of eight million people and could make new friends. New friends? I didn't have old friends.

"If I'm gonna get through this, I gotta go through this."

"That's better," I suddenly heard. "Son, why do you think I brought you through all this?"

"It's obvious you love me," was my unsure response. What was He trying to squeeze out of me?

"Not that My love is a small thing, but seriously, Dave, do you think it's all warm fuzzy love? Do you think I'm that single-faceted?"

"No. Not at all. I'm not sure what to do. I'm way up here. I have one friend within 1000 miles. I'm exhausted like you wouldn't believe!"

"Really? Technically, you are correct. It is not a matter of belief. Dave, I KNOW precisely how tired you are. Do you need a reminder of how I got you through that last night of the storm? I know exactly what you need and where you are."

"Father, I remember. I will never forget."

"I know you won't, but better than that, I Am Me. I don't fail—ever. I created you, and I Am making you into who I want you to be. Now, you agreed. You need to trust me. I've got this all worked out. I assure you it will rarely be the way you think it should be. Let's face it. You don't have the best track record when doing things independently. Sometimes, you'll feel things are impossible, but it will always be for your best and those around you."

"That sounds all fine and well, but what am I supposed to do now?"

"Dave, live your life! Get through every day. Look for the next thing to do with great expectations! I have a lot of things in store for you. If you do as I ask, you'll never want for anything. People will most certainly try to harm you. It comes with the territory, so stand firm in this relationship with Me. I'll always provide for you and show you how to get out if things turn against you. How's that for a commitment from Me?"

"It sounds great. How many people can say they've got you at their back?!"

I felt a displeased look.

"All of my children. Whether they understand it or not, I'm always there."

"Oh yeah. Sorry. I forget who I'm talking to sometimes."

"Dave, it's okay. Just don't forget you are incredibly special to Me, but so are the people you'll find in your path as you go on from here. Love them because I have loved you. Forgive them because I've forgiven you. Carry their burdens with them. Pray for them, and Dave, give because you will always have what you need no matter how much you give."

"How can I say 'no' to you? Never mind, don't answer that!" I sincerely heard a chuckle!

"See? You are teachable, after all! True, I had to do the whole storm thing, but you can indeed learn—hardheaded, stubborn, and indifferent at ..."

"Stop! I get it."

"Oh, I know, heh-heh-heh," He chuckled, "Just having some fun with you. You should lighten up some. Learn to enjoy what I've given you. Otherwise? Otherwise, you're wasting my efforts. Now, I'm just going to let that lay. Feel free to pick it up when you're ready."

He paused briefly and continued, "'What do you do?' I believe it is the question of the moment. Live, love, and serve. Walk forward. Live in the moment. Take what I give you and put your best effort into it. I love your improvement. It's that whole journey thing again. Let me know when you need Me. I'll be right here beside you anyhow."

"Lord? I Nee…"

Interrupting me, he said, "Yes? I know. You need Me. I have a sense of humor and appreciate your effort, but I know what you planned to do. It's kind of impossible to play a joke on Me."

I smiled, knowing He knew that I knew that He …. Well, never mind.

The sun had risen now on the bustling downtown Boston early morning scene, and I was struggling. Fatigue tinged with the discomfort and fear of unfamiliar territory brought back unbidden complaints.

Somewhere between genuine tears and childish whining, I mumbled half to myself and half to God,

"'Seize the moment,' He says. 'Find the joy!' Yeah right. And I know you hear me. I'm about out of steam! And I know you know that too!"

I shuffled miserably down the sidewalk, looked up, and lo-and-behold, a McDonald's was inside the other end of downtown Boston's bus station/commuter rail station. I could buy a large Diet Coke and a sausage biscuit for a dollar apiece! I had just enough left over!

Uh, that'd be a resounding "NO!"

Well, Toto, we're not in Georgia anymore! It was my first shot of culture shock. Two dollars and sixty-nine cents later, I had a Diet Coke, no sausage, no biscuit, just one lonely Diet Coke. And there would be no free refills, I discovered after quickly draining the cup! Ouch!

I didn't want to call Danielle too early, so I waited. So, beginning at 8:00 a.m., I started borrowing phones. I called every fifteen minutes.

No answer.

"Well, you've gotten yourself into a mess." Grumbling and moaning, I searched for a new person to accost to try Danielle again. 8:15, 8:30, 8:45, 9:00. Argh. How much more? What would I do? Despondent, I crumpled to the floor. Leaning back against a wall, I put my head in my hands.

I heard the sound of a throat clearing, "What now, Lord? Can't you see I'm trying to be miserable?"

"What was that, sir?"

Looking up, I realized a familiar man was standing before me. I'd used his phone earlier.

"Did you ever reach your friend?"

In complete embarrassment, I sputtered, "No. She still hasn't picked up."

Oh, I wasn't embarrassed that he heard me talking to God. I was embarrassed that he heard me talking to God like I did! He hadn't seemed to notice.

He said, "I'm about to catch an Uber. Before I do, would you like to use my phone again?"

I tried, she answered, and now, I was really embarrassed before God. Once again, my Father had sent me aid when I needed it at the right time, but once again, I was an idiot. I had every reason to trust God, and I was grumbling and moaning. It must be a long journey to arrive at the point of not groaning and lamenting. I still haven't gotten there despite all His interventions in my life.

And you don't know, but a fraction of it so far!

I wish you could write accents. If a classic "Southie" accent is a thing, Danielle has it! Look up "Southie" in the dictionary. Her picture is probably in the entry.

"Now, Dave, you're going to have to give me a few minutes. I got to get myself together. It will take me an hour and a half to get there on my scoota." Or something to that effect.

Danielle is my buddy. She's a real friend. It would only be after she arrived that I would discover she was extremely ill.

"Danielle, I hate for you to come so far."

"It's okay, Dave. I don't have much, but I've got a phone for you. It's just an Obama phone, but you can't do anything without a phone. You'll need a phone, so I've got to bring it to you. Can you get on the Red Line right there in the station and ride it to the end to Braintree?"

"Sure." I had no idea how I would ride the subway. I'd spent my last dime.

It wasn't hard to find the subway entrance. The gate beside the turnstiles was open, and people flowed through it.

"Thanks, Lord, you are amazing!"

I felt the glow of approval as I headed down the stairs. I boarded the Red Line for the first of hundreds of times before my relationship with the Red Line and my time in Massachusetts would end.

Struggling to keep my eyes open, I waited for Danielle's arrival. Was it a coincidence that Motel 6, where I worked when I met Danielle, was on the far side of the subway station complex? With the sputtering sound of a scooter cascading through the air, I thanked God the wait had not been too long.

"Now Dave, I brought'cha this phone. You can't do anything without a phone. And here's a Little Debbie. I don't have any money else I'd give you some," she said with a welcome Southie accent.

It was good to see a familiar face. It was good to feel like somebody cared, but on the other hand, I couldn't shake the feeling of being an ant in the middle of a shopping mall. I was tired. I was humanly alone. Boston was a new, enormous place with lots of concrete, asphalt, and buildings. Bostonian accents and culture surrounded me at every turn.

However, Danielle, even with that funky accent, was a sight for sore eyes, and these sore eyes saw she was ill.

"Danielle, I didn't care if you gave me anything. I'm just glad you're here, though I wish you'd told me you were sick! I would never have asked you to come to me."

"Now, Dave, I had to get you this phone, and you need some direction. You're my friend. I couldn't leave you hanging. So, let's start with where you need to go. I have a plan. Dave, you got to get plugged in. You need help."

With that, Danielle plunged into her plan. First, I needed to go to the hospital and tell them I was suicidal. She told me they'd keep me for a few days, but it would plug me into the system, and I could obtain the help I needed.

First off, I would never tell anybody I wanted to kill myself. I might have been in rough shape. I might have been despondent a few days prior, but there was no way I'd make those words out of my mouth—not with the way God had rescued me.

Secondly, this reeked of a scam. I'm not one to scam the government. The government didn't have any money. Its money came out of people's pockets. My pride just wouldn't let me participate.

"Live in the moment," He said. "Take what I give you," He said. Lying to a doctor would not be what God wanted me to do, but Danielle was a Godsend. I needed help. I needed some prescriptions, so the idea was not wholly off-kilter. Where was the balance?

I thanked Danielle profusely. What an act of kindness. What an incredible display of friendship! Danielle prayed for me. We prayed together. We ate our Little Debbies, and then I hurried her off. I had to decide, and I wouldn't be vertical much longer. I finally settled on heading to the hospital. It couldn't hurt.

Having seen Danielle off, I asked for directions and headed a couple of miles to the closest hospital.

I panicked as I neared. I saw the parking lot. It was empty, and visible signs of idleness were everywhere. It didn't necessarily look unkempt, and I should know what that looked like. All I had to do was look in the mirror.

I wouldn't make it to the next hospital. That was a given. There was nothing to do but round the building and check. Giving up seemed to be my only foreseeable option.

The first side is empty. The second side was bereft of people. To the point of shuffling, I turned the corner and saw an ambulance! Thank God, at least transportation to a staffed hospital was available!

Someone walked out of the door. I stumbled as I entered, and a nurse was at the desk.

Track 8: Rest

The title says it all. Sometimes, you have to rest. There is much more to rest than lying in a hospital bed. I was certainly in need of physical rest. The mind and spirit also require a time-out. I had been running for my life and suffering before the walk began.

I'm pretty stubborn and hardheaded, though. It is quite a statement that God would take me through a storm to rearrange my faith, desires, and life. It is a statement about the condition of my heart. It also says much about how far God will go for an errant soul.

He is called the Good Shepherd for a reason.

I needed rest, and I got it. I would need more. I would spend many months in rehab for my hand, counseling sessions, and in the Dentist's chair, having 24 broken teeth dug out of infected gums.

I had a road ahead I still had to travel, but I would go down that road with a different frame of mind and spirit. I had discovered the best kind of rest— resting in Christ.

"Whoever dwells in the shelter of the Most High will rest in the shadow of the Almighty. I will say of the LORD, 'He is my refuge and my fortress.'"

Psalm 91:1,2 (NIV)

****

"Sir, you need some help," again, not so much of a question. It was more of a declaration, much the same as the lady at the health club a thousand miles away now and seemingly years ago.

"I need help" was about all I squeezed out.

"Come sit down!" she said, escorting me to a chair with a worried look on her face.

Determined to find some help and not to lie to do it, I said, "I've been struggling." My mind bent more to the physical. She interpreted it psychologically.

"No worries. Come with me," the nurse led me to a heavenly bed.

Whatever worries I had about my ability to acquire help would disappear in the clanging alarms of an automated blood pressure machine!

Being in the right place, the hospital, was a good thing. After all, I had been through, lying on a real bed allowed me to think. God had met me where I was in a pretty fantastic way. He had never left me, and returning to Him was simple; a broken heart, a prayer, and a song worked.

The only thing that had complicated matters was me, my stubbornness, and my sin. I needed time to soak it all in.

I was about to have some of that commodity.

"Let's check your vitals!"

My reverie was interrupted by a triage nurse in the small, partially unused hospital in Quincy, Massachusetts. Rolling the blood pressure machine next to me, she hooked me up to a pulse oximeter on the left index finger and a cuff on the upper right arm. Within moments, the alarm sounds filled the room!

"Sir, do you have any cardiac history at all?"

"Yes, ma'am."

"Just lay there. I'll be right back."

I was drifting into near unconsciousness when a voice drew me back to reality,

"Sir… Sir!" Blasted pesky nurses!

"Yes, ma'am?"

"I need you to take this and try to calm down as much as possible. We're definitely keeping you. This hospital is just an emergency facility now. We're going to have to transfer you to a hospital. We want to help, but where we transfer you to depends on getting control of your vitals. Take this and try to stay calm."

Calm? That was easy enough. Add two days in a storm plus nine-and-a-half hours waiting on a bus, plus thirty hours traveling in a Greyhound, plus 12 more hours combined with a hospital bed, blankets, and pillow. Yeah, I was out like a light in about sixty seconds!

Interrupted again, I wished they would just let me rest!

"Sir, I hate to wake you, but you've been asleep for 18 hours, and I must get your vital signs."

"We've been monitoring you, but you needed rest. The doctor told us to let you sleep."

As I groggily sat in bed, the nurse strapped me to the machine, and the alarms began clanging again. My blood pressure was 160/135, and my resting heart rate was 153. These results were after the medication from the night before and eighteen hours of sleep.

My resting heart rate should've been around 70 bpm, and my blood pressure should have been about 120/80. As it stood, my blood pressure was dangerously high, but my heart rate was catastrophically high. That was a terrible combination. At my age, the highest my heart rate should be in any situation is in the neighborhood of 167 (220 minus my age). A trip to the bathroom would have elevated my heart above that. While trying to reassure me—no panic allowed, the nurse called for the doctor. The doctor's clinical diagnosis was "bad shape!" Of course, they had other words, but that'll work here.

"We've got to lower both and quickly!" the doctor declared, after which I was duly shot and pilled.

"You came here for help, and we'll give it to you, but we cannot transport you the way things are."

Even with the previous meetings with God and His promise to me, I was concerned. I will not tell a lie. When a doctor is handling you with kid gloves, and everybody else is running around with concerned looks abounding, it's next to impossible to maintain one's composure.

Every few minutes, the nurse would check my stats. Medication doing its job, we watched the numbers begin to drop until they reached 140/100 at 120 beats per minute and stopped falling.

"I'm afraid to give you any more medication. There may be a delayed effect, and we gave you enough that you should be bottoming out about now. I deem you safe enough to transport. Your EKG is abnormal, but that fits with your cardiac history. They'll probably dose you again when you arrive at the hospital."

He continued after a short pause, "You need to watch this. You were too close to another heart attack. You need to understand this clearly. To hear this is probably stressful, but do not let yourself stress until this is under control!"

Visions of the storm danced before my eyes, and I chuckled inwardly. One more evident sign that my Father had everything under control. I hadn't died yet, and He'd told me He had a plan. I trusted Him. Why not? He'd just proved He'd had His hand on my heart the whole time.

The transport gurney rolled in. The ambulance ride to the "full-service" hospital was uneventful.

The doctor was insightful and quick to point out the obvious. I may have been diabetic and had a cardiac condition, but I, like the physician in front of me, knew those were not at the root of my current issues.

"Looking at your chart, I must tell you, you are exhibiting classic signs of PTSD. I know nothing about you, but something is happening in your life, and if we do not handle it, it will kill you—literally. I don't know how much they told you over in Quincy (pronounced Quinzee, for the uninitiated in Boston-speak), but you were about this close (finger and thumb separated by the thickness of a sheet of paper) to being dead. I don't want you freaking out on me, but you better help me figure this out. I've got you on so much medication right now that some would be in a coma, yet your heart rate is still above 100 bpm."

"Well, the short answer is I spent close to a year working undercover in Georgia, running about ninety miles an hour, seven days a week, and twenty-four hours a day. I had multiple attempts on my life—one of which broke bones—injuries to my leg, arm, and back, concussion, all my teeth kicked down my throat, crushed my left hand, and they kept kicking until they heard sirens coming down the road. Thank God I don't remember most of it, but I did manage to drive away from the ordeal, although I don't remember that part."

He stared at me for a full minute, discerning the truth of the matter.

"Well, that would certainly do it! You're going to need some help with that. Your best answer is therapy. You will have to work your way back out of this psychological hole. And it will take real work. I will keep you here as long as you want to stay, and I'll help you find a therapist when you leave. We're not set up for that here, and I highly recommend some medication, at least until you leave, so I'm prescribing it. Taking it is your choice, but you won't make it without it. I cannot stress how important this is to your very survival."

Everything in the hospital was a complete blur after two days into my stay. I don't know if the meds were helping or not. I was never awake long enough to tell.

"Look, Doc., I can't do this. I'm never conscious. I'll be asleep again in five minutes."

"Too heavy for you? We can adjust the dosage, but you're on an extremely light dose."

"I'm already only taking half of what you prescribed."

"Has it occurred to you that your exhaustion plays a part in this? I don't know everything, obviously, but from the little you told me, it could be many months before you're even close to recovery. The meds are leveling out some of your neurotransmitters that have gone haywire. It will take time to heal. It would help if you forgot some of the things you've gone through, and you shouldn't worry so much about the future. That'll take care of itself."

He continued, "Have you given any real consideration to enjoying each moment you live? So relax. Personal growth isn't always about tomorrow. More often than not, it is about filling up your days in ways that help you move forward, but it is not about where you'll be; it's about where you are. It's about the moments in which you live. So, grab each moment and wring your life out of it!"

I smiled as I said, "Somebody told me the same thing just a few days ago."

"Really? Who?"

"You'd probably not believe me."

"Must be pretty smart."

"You have no idea. At any rate, I'm stopping the psych meds. I can't think. I can't stay awake. I can't function. I'll take the rest of the medications, but I'm dropping those."

I walked out of the little room and back into my room, laid down, and woke up twenty hours later. I hate to admit it, but maybe I was just beyond exhaustion.

But now I was awake. I still wasn't ready for my usual limited sleep of four hours a night, but being awake in the hospital was for the birds! It was Monday afternoon.

Ironically, exactly eight days to the minute from when I left Griffin, Georgia, seeking escape and freedom, I was talking to my nurse about escaping the hospital, and she was doing her best to talk me out of it,

"David, you can barely stand on your feet. You need several more days at least."

"I'm feeling trapped. I'm about as nervous as I can be. I'm about to go crazy in here." That last one was funny, considering I was voluntarily in a psych ward. Of course, one might argue I'd already arrived at crazy, but I digress.

"Well, you don't need to go anywhere today. You have nowhere to go. Stay tonight and talk to your doctor in the morning."

"I'm not trying to argue. I'm just ready to go. But, of course, I can wait 'til the morning." Better sense had briefly seized my mind. I grabbed a newspaper crossword puzzle, lay on my bed to do it, and promptly fell asleep before answering the first one. A nurse came by, took the pen and paper from my hands, and laid them on my nightstand. I awoke twelve hours later. Hardheaded and stubborn to my detriment?

Absolutely! It's still somewhat true, although I have improved considerably since then.

I was chompin' at the bit by the time my doctor rolled in.

"David, I told you you could leave when ready. I think you're far from ready. Would you consider a few more days?"

"No."

He looked expectantly at me, hoping for something more.

Look, I'm the consummate salesman. I used to train salespeople, and I was pretty good at it. Handling objections can come in a myriad of forms. I can manipulate words with the best of them and sway the opinions of most. Objections are reasons not to do something that could be satisfied.

Someone might say, "I don't have the money right now." Answer: "Well, if I split those payments up or delay your first payment until next month, can you take delivery today?"

Or,

"I don't think the color is right for my kitchen." Answer: "Ma'am, I've failed you. I'm so sorry! We have more colors. Doesn't this look great against your curtains?"

Those were objections. They were seeking information they did not have, and I needed to provide more. The only answer I ever dreaded from a customer was an emphatic "No." "No, but…" I could deal with it, but a simple no is a rejection, not an objection. I'm aware of the communication rules!

The first to speak loses, so as my "no" hung alone in the air, I sat and smiled at the doctor's expectant face.

Still silently smiling at the doctor, my "no" had finally drifted to the floor.

"Well, okay, let me put your release papers together. Now, David, you're homeless."

All of creation came to a halt. Those words split the air again, first heard at the QT on Hamilton Mill Parkway in Georgia.

"You're homeless."

I'm not sure if the doctor had punched me, it would have hit me with more devastation. It's not that I didn't realize it. There's just something that makes your entire insides shrivel up in despair, hearing those words. I'll not lie. I almost changed my mind about leaving.

"You can not survive outside, so you must go to a shelter. I'll include a list of all the shelters in your release papers. You'll have to choose one, and we'll get you a ride."

The doctor left the room, leaving me to worry about where I would go. My reverie was interrupted by a nurse I'd not seen in my five days of care.

"I understand you're homeless."

Boy, I sure wished people would stop saying that. It drove a stake into my soul with each utterance.

"Yes, ma'am."

"The doctor will give you a list of shelters. On second thought, don't even worry about it. Where you need to go is the Salvation Army Shelter in Cambridge. Don't worry about it. I'll handle it."

She bustled out of the room, and about fifteen minutes later, she came back. With her, she brought my official release papers, my current prescriptions, and one brand new one.

"Here is the doctor's order for you to go to the Salvation Army in Cambridge. We'll call an Uber when you're packed and ready."

Of course, part of the beauty of Uber is you don't have to know how to get somewhere. You don't even have to know where you are. That's a good thing because though I'd been to Boston before, I didn't know where Cambridge was, much less where I'd find the Salvation Army Cambridge Corps. My Uber ride dropped me off at the door of the shelter.

"My name is Mark. Let me get you to fill out some paperwork." He was a friendly and wonderfully polite man in the Salvation Army Shelter office.

It is difficult for me to write about our first meeting. He's "Marky-Mark," and I'll always be "Davey-Dave" to him. Was there anyone who would have been a better first contact? I think not! As our nicknames suggest, we became friends. He is everything you'd want him to be in his position—kind, compassionate, and a stickler for the rules, but not so much so that he wasn't willing and able to work around issues to help somebody. He is smart with a certain amount of charisma. Everyone loves Mark!

I had a problem because the shelter needed my picture ID. I didn't have one. I had known I would need ID when I left home. I had my birth certificate and my social security card, but I had no picture ID. Mark explained I should go to the Massachusetts RMV and secure it the next day. Since I was coming from the hospital, they'd give me a day to acquire the ID.

The following day, I was out the door. I obtained a bus pass and went to the nearest Massachusetts RMV. I strolled into the Watertown Mall and turned the corner to view the ever-so-typical long line in every state I've ever been!

Well, I expected the line. I had almost everything I needed. I had all the paperwork except the green kind. Someone had told me they thought there was a program to help folks like me with their IDs. I just had to have faith. God didn't bring me this far to drop me! I was bold, though humbled. Everything would be all right.

Yeah, right! The government was involved. Something was bound to go wrong. I got to the front of the line, where a woman was reviewing documents before I could even take a number.

"Sir, your birth certificate is not acceptable. It needs a raised stamp on it, and we used to have a program to help with IDs, but the state stopped it."

The look on my face must've matched the sinking action of my heart.

"Sir, maybe they can help you at the help desk." I think she was genuinely concerned for me.

The only problem? I got the same answer from the woman at the help desk, who then pushed me to the on-site manager.

Well, this wasn't progressing. I'm pretty familiar with how things work. No's generally become firmer the further up the chain you go, but you have to ask if there's any hope.

"Father, I need some help here."

There was no verbal answer, but I'd already figured out He's more of a doer. More often than not, His actions speak volumes all the books in the world could not contain! So, I waited to talk with the manager.

"Mr. Riordan, they told you the right thing, but let me look at what you have, and I'll see if I can do anything."

I cringed as I spoke, "Ma'am, I have another problem. I don't have the twenty-five dollars either."

She stared and said, "I don't think I can do anything. Let me see, and then we'll worry about that."

Forty-five minutes later, I left the RMV with a Massachusetts ID. I do not know what else she did, but she paid the fee for my ID out of her pocket! I've seen plenty of miracles, but this one was amazing. God has continually put the right people before me at the right time. My friends are as amazed as I am. This kind of thing doesn't happen! I hadn't schmoozed here, no smooth-talking, just a plea to my Father.

That's right. My Father was involved, and He never fails!

The next thing I needed to do was to have a checkup with a doctor. Housed in the shelter facility is a clinic from a great organization, Healthcare for the Homeless. I signed up for a visit with the PA and waited for my turn. Another soon-to-be friend walked out and called my name.

"My name is Erlinda. The first thing we need to do is apply for insurance. That's one of the things I do."

We talked as she entered my information.

"Wait, a minute, have you lived in Massachusetts before? And how long have you been here?"

It was Wednesday, "Six days, and no, ma'am. I've only visited a few years back for work." I had no idea what she was getting at.

"You have insurance," she said, startled. "Look here! How in the world did you get insurance activated the day you arrived?"

"I have no idea. I answered some questions when I arrived at the hospital but never applied." I arrived at the hospital at about 2:00 p.m.

"Yes, well, that office closes at four or five o'clock, and it was activated that day. I don't even know what somebody could do to make it happen so quickly, and I know the system well. Somebody did something for you."

Looking at me in a new light, Erlinda ushered me into my next hero, Deb Sarsen, PA, who became very important to me as the summer wore on.

Track 9: Waves and Winds

Waves and Winds is a reworking of the hymn "Be Still My Soul," written by Katharina von Schlegel in 1697.

The words impacted me deeply as they reminded me of the sovereignty of God that brings peace and steadfastness. I felt the need to weave both a sense of hope and desperation throughout the song musically, a reflection of the journey of the Christian experience. Jesus is leading us to Himself, and no matter our circumstances, He knows that our most profound joy is only found in Him.

-Timothy-

"My soul, wait in silence for God alone, for my expectation is from Him. He alone is my rock and my salvation, my fortress where I will not be shaken."

Psalm 62:5,6 (WEB)

****

May 6, 2018—10:00 a.m.

I contemplated my new life as I sat in the Salvation Army Church on my second Sunday in Massachusetts. I had been here for ten days, and my feet were on the ground, although I wasn't exactly running. The truth is, I should have stayed longer in the hospital, but Father had my back, as He had promised. It was a new world for me. Everything was different.

Oh, I still had issues, but my perspective had changed.

"Son, this new thing you have is called faith, real faith, life-altering faith. It is My gift to you. Seize life. I like what the doctor told you. 'Wring the life out of every moment.' I kind of helped him with that one. I wanted you to remember it. Follow my lead. I've given you the story you've long desired. Write it down. I have some things in store for the rest of your life."

Gently scolding, He continued, "Now, quit daydreaming and listen to the lesson. This one's just for you, and be prepared; I've got something to show you afterward. Talk to the Majors. They are now your pastors and will not steer you wrong!"

As I tuned into the teaching, Major Tom Babbitt began speaking from Judges 16 from the story of Samson, "And the hair on his head began to grow again." Yep, a message just for me!

I introduced myself to Major Tom Bab-bitt, and we talked about the possibility of my playing the piano. He told me to keep on coming back.

I did.

It would be a couple of months when Major Bessie told me she'd been praying for a pianist before I would connect the dots. After all, I had a doctor's prescription to go to the Salvation Army Shelter and a free Uber ride. I was a pianist, and God had once again moved. It was one of those unrecognized miracles. I see them all the time, but rarely when they happen.

Settling in at the shelter was challenging. However, by the second week in Massachusetts, I had a library card secured with my new ID. I found the amply supplied computer room and began to obey the Lord's command,

"Write it down."

As I was penning my story, my brother was reading along as I wrote—the brother who gave me his last fifteen dollars as I left Griffin, Georgia,

"Dave, the book needs a 'Eureka!' moment near the end."

I smiled inside. The life I now live is one Eureka moment after another. My Heavenly Father has called me out, set me apart, and surrounds me daily. My life has changed to Biblical proportions! It has been one miracle after another, and I can't wait to tell you all about it. The next book is currently being lived!

****

End Note

At the time of the above events, I only sometimes recognized what was happening. Isn't that the way it is typically? We rarely appreciate a miracle when it's taking place because we don't notice the intricacy of God's hand until later. I was in the middle of God's miraculous hand moving in my life!

Miracles unseen? How many cataclysmic tsunamis missed the Ark while Noah, his family, and the animals were tucked safely within the boat? How many blows, meant to kill, slightly changed trajectory, leaving Paul with yet another testimony? Better yet, didn't the disciples misunderstand the miracle of the crucifixion as it was taking place?

Horror changes to pure joy as we examine this thing called miraculous living. Noah had to endure the flood, Paul the beatings, and our Savior had to overcome the cross and death. Victory always comes in the morning after the darkest of nights!

And we have been made more than conquerors through Christ, Who overcame sin, death, and the grave. How can we conquer if there's nothing to overcome and nothing to defeat? If we never faced hardship, would we ever learn of our need for Him? In our quest to fill that need, oh, how much more we find when we rest in Him!

Life often comes at us a million miles an hour, and by necessity, we must face life on life's terms, with complete reliance on God. There is no other successful life strategy!

I'm afraid I've spent far too much of my life sitting inside my own Ark, wondering why I must endure the storm! I've failed to be grateful for all the destructive waves that merely passed by. I have been unable to understand there is an end to the deluge and that the storms are only temporary.

So, for today, I will commit to enduring the storm and marvel at the waves that pass me by. And, for today, I will bask in the promise of coming sunlight. On this, it is faith. It is the sure knowledge there is an end, for I have been promised an Abundant Life by One Who never lies!

It is good I boast of my trials, for in those trials, I find patience, the knowledge that experience brings, and hope built upon all of that. It is this hope that cannot be restrained. It resonates with those who would hear me, for who is not seeking the Hope of Life? I have become a soda that has been shaken—no, better yet, a volcano bursting from its earthly bonds—a soul who has found relief!

I would be remiss not to proclaim, "Christ made the way. It is yours for the asking!

He is awaiting your call!!

In Christ Alone,
the Bread
(A Product of the Loving Baker)

Track 10: Sound of the Rivers

Every movie needs a great song playing as the credits roll!

Okay, so this isn't a movie, and all the credit goes to our Father in Heaven—no need to roll past that.

Dan and Timothy would wholeheartedly agree. Working with them and many others has been incredible to produce this work that goes beyond a typical reading experience. I have repeatedly told people how cool it is to be a part of this. Their response has usually been incredulous, "It's your story. You're not just a part!" My response has been one full of gratefulness, for there would be no stories without the Author and Finisher of our faith. There would be no music without the Composer of Hearts.

"It is not my story. It is His story!" And, to Him, I say, as this song says, "Your Majesty is blowing my mind!"

"Your works declare the glory of Your Kingdom and speak of Your might, to make known to the sons of men Your mighty acts and the Glory of the Majesty of Your Kingdom."

Psalm 145:11-12 (NASB)

The Baker's Story
My Saga

Book 3

Who I Have Become

OR

Unrecognizable

OR

A New Kind of Life!

Coming
after a few more miracles

Look for more from David on Amazon:

The Baker: Prelude to a New Kind of Life

The stand-alone story of the four
most consequential days of his life.

The Seed The Gardener And the Servant

An illustrated book on the hope of Eternity
and a stirring memorial.

Forty Days of Prayer for the Forgotten Ones Crusade

A Baker's Dozen

Thirteen weeks of devotionals
based on the Baker and the Bread blogs.

And of course, keep up with the
Crusade and read more daily content
on the New Baker and the Bread
on Facebook.

Coming Soon!!

Defeating the Darkness
A Graphic Novel

(Loosely based on the story of Job
for young adults).

Defeating the Darkness

Part I: The Setup

The throne room was packed; it was wall to wall, standing room only! Studies completed, observations made, and reports prepared, messengers arrived from throughout the kingdom.

The King spoke, "I want to know where you've been and what you've seen - from your perspectives." One by one, messengers from near and far presented their portfolios, discussed issues and lobbied for their solutions.

****

"All is well," Gavair smiled to himself, "I have been blessed way beyond what I deserve!"

He had started small. He had had no great inheritance, for his father had barely struggled through life financially. Spiritually, growing up, their family was wealthy! “Priorities,” his father often proclaimed, “Keep God first, and you’ll never lack for anything.

With profits from his first crop, he had purchased a ram and an ewe. Those two had become a flock. From earnings at the market, he had purchased a couple of head of cattle that had grown into a herd. He had bought and tamed land. He found a wonderful woman to marry. Flocks, herds, and now his “litter” of children had all prospered!

All because he had followed what his father had insisted was right. He was profoundly grateful. He never missed an opportunity to thank God for all he had. He had worked hard, but so did other people, and their priorities not being the same had not been blessed as Gavair had. There was no question in his mind from Whom all this goodness had come.

Gavair made his way to his private chapel. He had a few minutes. He wanted to spend them with the Father. He was just so grateful!

****

“Your most high Majesty,” the words dripping off his tongue like honey with a bitter aftertaste, Ma-ashim took his place in front of the King. He was last, but it had been intentional. He took great pride in rocking the boat, and on this day, he had finally concocted a way to get under the skin of the King.

"So, waited 'til last, Ma-ashim? What's going on, and where all have you been?"

"I have been following Your commands, oh my liege!" dark undercurrents oozing unseen around his words. "I have taken great interest in Your kingdom, my Lord, and all of Your subjects. Curious people, your subjects. I find it intriguing to observe them. Very interesting, to say the least!"

"I am quite fond of them, you know? They are interesting. I'm glad you've been watching. In all of your observations, did you notice one particular man? His name is Gavair. He is really something. He gets this whole thing. He prospers because he does the one thing I asked of all my subjects! He maintains My priorities. He and I have a pretty good relationship."

"Yeah. About that. I have seen Gavair. Don't You think You've got it all backward? You have a good relationship with him because You have been so generous. I'm not so sure his motives are as pure as what you say."

"Careful, now, Ma-ashim, are you suggesting I cannot read a man's heart?"

Face averted downward – more to hide his smirk and contempt for the King and His Kingdom, Ma-ashim responded, “Why, no, my Lord, I would never presume to pass any judgment on you. It is a statement about us and your other subjects.”

“Really? Do tell,” the King didn’t bother to hide His contempt for the head messenger, for He indeed had no trouble discerning the workings of anyone’s heart.

Bent upon delivering a personal blow to the King, Ma-ashim missed the verbal and nonverbal cues and continued with his machinations, “Ah, most exquisite One, your Beneficence is so great, some of us here cannot see as you do, and we do not understand these great matters of the human heart. It’s not so much about Your discernment as our ability to understand Your greatest achievement! We are simply looking to learn something of these things if You can but show us. I don’t see how Gavair could feel any other way than he does with all You do for him.”

“I provide for Gavair, and he is grateful. While I certainly appreciate his gratitude, an important part of our interactions, his gratitude is not the foundation of our relationship. I have faith in Gavair. He would still be my loyal subject and friend if he lost everything.”

Glee, hidden behind a blank face, Ma-ashim reveled as he saw the proverbial trap tittering on the verge of snapping shut. “Your Munificence knows his heart so much better than we. Are you sure?”

That last question hung in the air with uncertain power. All other sounds in the hall ceased. All eyes in the room turned toward the King. Time stood still. No one had ever pushed so far with the King. Half of the room anticipated the sure reprisal from the King.

The other half had grown curious during the exchange. Like Ma-ashim, they wondered to themselves. What would subjects like Gavair do without the King's ample provision? What would he do if his fortune were reversed? No one had ever seemingly taunted the King as the messenger had, but now the desire to know an answer permeated the King's throne room. For many, the desire was merely academic. For a few, they shared a distaste for how the King treated his subjects in general.

They were servants desiring to be subjects - and maybe even more.

The King chuckled - not a necessarily happy sound - with a severe look on his face, "Hmm. You will see a heart of faith and, perhaps, learn from it. Do what you will, but do not harm the man!"

BAM! The imagined sound reverberated in Ma-ashim's mind. The trap had slammed shut. He was jubilant. This was awesome. It was about time the King and His prized subjects were put in their places! Not only would he shame them all, he knew a more significant battle was being fought in the minds in the ranks of the messengers of the King!

Bowing and scraping, Ma-ashim could barely contain his malignant joy! If the King had any concept of just how devious Ma-ashim could be, the King would be afraid!! By the time he was done with Gavair, nothing would be left of the man's psyche - much less his so-called faith!

Ma-ashim strode from the palace. He had made his plan, worked it, and set the snare. The idiot King had faith in a simple man. The messenger's goal was within reach, and the King was now trapped.

Ma-ashim just knew it!

*** To be Continued!! ***

Just a Man and the Accuser (for that is what the latter name means in Hebrew): each plays a role in this story that begins in this episode and will stretch into several upcoming graphic novels. In the beginning, Gavair is unknowingly pulled into the plot of the Accuser. If the story sounds familiar, it should. Obviously, I loosely based the story on Job.

Our relationship with God is not based on prosperity, health, or anything tangible. Trust, gratitude, and hope are all components of a good relationship but are not the foundation. As with any other relationship, as we get to know our Father, those things grow, as do our faith and love. It is well said that as we experience the Father and get to know Him, we find Him to be worth it all. It is a value above all others.

To know Him is to love Him. To know Him is to trust Him; out of that trust grows a faith that cannot be shaken! Faith is the sure knowledge that God will do what He says because He has always done what He said He would do. We discover this to be accurate as we experience God!

God does not expect you to worship Him blindly nor know Him abstractly. He expects you to experience Him – to get to know Him. You cannot know Him without spending time with Him.

He is awaiting your call!!

In Christ Alone,
The Bread
(A Product of the Loving Baker)

****

ABOUT THE AUTHOR

See page 1

But seriously, David began writing immediately upon arriving in Massachusetts and serving the Lord in any capacity he could: volunteering in the Harvard Square Meals program and as a worship leader with his church, the Cambridge Salvation Army Corps.

After God called him to Austin, TX, he built a successful independent ministry to the Forgotten Ones around him while being an active member of the Connection Church in Buda, TX.

The Baker and the Bread Ministries has grown to be an international team of volunteers seeking to serve those less remembered by society and the church: the homeless, disenfranchised, and disconnected.

David continues to publish daily on the New Baker and the Bread on Facebook while posting simultaneously to X, Instagram, YouTube, and LinkedIn.

With God-given compassion for the lost and hurting, David is currently on a multi-year trek across the U.S. to reach the Forgotten Ones.

ABOUT THE COMPOSERS
Dan Riordan

Dan graduated from Mercer University with a BA in Music Composition. He received his master's from Southwestern Theological Seminary. Composing music is nothing new for him. He has written and directed musicals and cantatas for the churches he has served for years.

Highly skilled as an instrumentalist, he, alone plays every instrument for his compositions on the Baker Prelude Soundtrack.

When not composing, Dan and his wife, Laurie, are constructing a house on their property in Southwest Georgia, where he is attempting to grow much of his own food. And, when not talking to his little brother on the phone, he enjoys the freedom of riding his motorcycle and hiking.

For more outstanding music from Dan, go to
youtube.com/watch?v=7Ijz6TsOkVk

Dan may be contacted at
mountainscape7@gmail.com

Timothy Riordan

After graduating from Liberty University, Timothy passed on the opportunity for a possible recording contract. Instead, he and his wife, Jillian, self-funded a year-long mission trip to Birmingham, England. While there, Timothy and Jillian supported the local church through pastoral care, serving the community and spreading the name and mission of Jesus. He and his band, Atlas Rhoads, also used their music as an avenue of ministry and successfully toured Europe and Israel with their unique sound and message of Jesus Christ.

Timothy moved to Charlotte, N.C., to serve as worship pastor at a local church for three years before he returned to his alma mater, where he now runs a recording studio for the Liberty Worship Collective. His days consist of recording originals for the team, songwriting, and mentoring the students in the band.

Timothy composed four of the songs on the Baker Prelude soundtrack. The rich tones of his vocals and striking guitar style are unmistakably Timothy. His background as a cellist also influences him, lending to a symphonic sound in his Indie-style compositions. You may find more of His music on Spotify, YouTube, and all other streaming platforms, and you can follow their journey on Instagram, as well, under @AtlasRhoads.

He is awaiting your call!!